$$P = d.t$$

OUTLINE OF A THEORY OF POWER

OF POWER

Jorge Majfud

HUMANUS

SAN DIEGO-ACAPULCO

P = d.t. Outline of a Theory of Power
ISBN: 978-1-956760-20-0
© Jorge Majfud 2023-2024
P = d.t. Bosquejo de una teoría del poder
jmajfud@ju.edu
© Illegal Humanus, January 2025
humanus.info
editor@humanus.com

TABLE OF CONTENTS

AN EQUATION OF THE HISTORY OF POWER

IN THIS BRIEF OUTLINE of an analysis of the history of power, we can observe a frequent and consistent pattern that runs through different periods, economic systems, and cultures, which can be synthesized into a minimal and simple equation, but with various derivations:

$$P = d.t$$

where P is the hegemonic power (it does not need to be an absolute power to be a dictatorial power); d represents dissent towards P, diversity (cultural, ideological, political, economic) and *freedom of expression*; and t signifies the tolerance of that power towards d.

If we solve for t, we have

$$t = P/d$$

which leads us to deduce that, as *dissent-diversity-freedom of expression* (d) increases in a given social system, tolerance (t) decreases, unless power (P) increases in the same proportion. A weakened or challenged dominant P, with alternatives or due to a changing social context, has a low level of tolerance towards dissent in all its forms. A hegemonic power without real opposition adorns its Pax Romana with greater tolerance that confirms its legitimacy among both its own and outsiders.

Naturally, this is a logic that refers to power equilibriums. It is a zero-sum equilibrium

$$P - d.t = 0$$

From there, we can ask, what happens when the equation fails to close to zero? The answer is a conjecture derived directly from the formula: in that case, we are facing a revolution where one order replaces (violently, according to Thucydides' Trap) another, and after a transition $P_a = P_c$ a new order is established: $P_c > P_a$ with a role reversal. Then, following the original formula,

$$d_c.t_c > d_a.t_a$$

Both a hegemonic power in decline and a hegemonic power on the rise will be governed by the same formula $P = d.t$, but the clash between the two conflicting systems cannot withstand the balance of the formula (for example, $Pa - d.t = 3$ or $Pc - d.t = -2$).

TOLERANT, AS LONG AS POWER DOES NOT TREMBLE

IF WE JUDGE THE FIRST CENTURY of our Era by the biblical accounts (real, imaginary, or distorted by repetition and convenience), we will always see the same dynamic. Jesus was crucified by the political establishment of a dominant Jewish class in complicity with the empire of the time, which allowed freedom of expression and freedom of religion as long as the disorder did not question its political hegemony in the colony. With the rise of Christianity and the subsequent decline of the Empire, persecution and intolerance towards these (d) dissenters increased until the breaking point of the early 4th century.

Both Jesus and other subversives of the time (from the Zealots to the *sicarii* or assassins, both considered terrorists for opposing the empire's occupation with violence) challenged the power pyramid in different ways, which led to the resolution being a summary trial and a political execution with the same method that was then used to execute criminals. The bad example of Jesus lay in a nonviolent challenge to the

$$P - d.t = 0$$

power of the rich and powerful and to social injustices, something quite common in the tradition of the so-called prophets of the Bible and, therefore, especially dangerous. In the case of anti-colonial resistance, it was something feared by the powers that be with greater perplexity than armed resistance.

The same can be said of the political execution of Socrates four centuries earlier, when his dissent touched the most sensitive nerves of the Athenian democracy's power. Socrates was accused of corrupting the youth with too many questions (his method of maieutics or "midwifery") and for his excessive doubts about the dominant gods of Athens.

Among the periods of greatest intolerance in Europe are those where the dominant power was questioned or threatened. Europe radiates an image of civilization, peace, and freedom, but its history of obsessive and continuous violence says exactly the opposite. In the Middle Ages, its fanaticism manifested in the Crusades "against the infidel" (the political and intellectual power of the time: the Muslim world) and in the Inquisition, a paradigm of intolerance toward dissent and freedom of expression. The brutality of this ideological police (the origin of modern police and of secret agencies like the CIA or the NSA) had different moments and, in all cases, was a response by

the power to new threats of opinion. From the persecution of Cathars and Waldensians in the 12th century, the intolerance of Spanish Catholicism during
the so-called Reconquista (which contrasted with
greater tolerance from the hegemonic power at the
time, the Islamic world, its main enemy), to the struggle against the new heretics, the Protestants and their
subversive reform of the 16th century.

Now, if we jump to the 20th century and another
center of "The free world" and a media example of
"Open society", we will observe the dynamics of P =
dt at different moments. For example, with the reaction of the anti-immigrant laws of 1924, no longer
against the Chinese who in the 19th century threatened to contaminate the blood and Anglo-Saxon
power, but against the darker-skinned Southern Europeans who, aside from representing an inferior
race, were workers bringing the contamination of socialist or anarchist ideas. By the 1920s and 1930s,
these new undesirables were anti-fascists expelled
from Italy, Germany, and Spain, threatening the Nazi
popularity among the great businessmen of the
United States.

If we set aside World War II (which deserves its
own chapter) and continue with the Cold War in the
United States, we will see the phenomenon of Mc-

Carthyism and its restrictions on freedom of expression as a direct result of a power insecure about its own strength, despite its privileged position, derived from World War II and due to the undeniable economic, social, and geopolitical achievements of its former ally and new default enemy—Anglo-Saxon fever cannot live without an enemy and it cannot live with one either—: the Soviet Union.

Outside the United States, in its southern colonies, the reality was even more unstable. Freedom of expression (freedom only when it is insignificant and controlled when it becomes significant) is characteristic of consolidated empires. Tolerance of the other (especially the other who thinks differently and challenges the dominant power) is typical of systems that cannot be threatened by freedom of expression or by dissent, but quite the opposite: when popular opinion has been crystallized, either by tradition or by mass propaganda, the opinion of the majority is the best form of legitimization. This is why these systems, always dominant, always imperial, do not grant their colonies the same rights they grant to their citizens. The numerous banana republic dictatorships imposed by imperial democracies are just one example that follows this logic. We will explain further later.

Now let us review the (2) legal aspect, the second rung of controlling dogma after (1) harassment, discrediting, and demonization of the dissident and before (3) police or military intervention where necessary, whether in the form of dictatorshipsmilitary or proxy wars, as is the case of the last three, two of which are already underway to crush any questioning of the dogma of power: Ukraine and Gaza —Taiwan or the South China Sea would be the third, which we analyzed almost two decades ago, when the world was distracted by "the Islamic threat." When the United States was in its infancy and fighting for its survival, its government did not hesitate to pass a law that prohibited any criticism of the government under the excuse of spreading false ideas and information—seven years after passing the famous First Amendment, which did not arise from religious tradition but from European anti-religious enlightenment. Naturally, that law of 1798 was called the Sedition Act. More than a century later, another law also called the Sedition Act, that of 1918, was passed as soon as there was popular resistance against the propaganda organized by masters like Edward Bernays in favor of intervening in the First World War—and thus ensuring the collection of European debts and (according to other theories) as bargaining currency in negotiating the handover of Palestine to the growing Zionist movement, a betrayal that turned the country most open to Jewish tradition, Germany, into an anti-Semitic machine. But this would be a topic for another book.

Let us return to the United States. In 1894, after the national strike crushed by the U.S. Army, the unionist Eugene Debs paid for his social activism with six months in prison, where he began to study socialist theory and, in 1901, founded the Socialist Party of America, managing to receive six percent of the vote in the 1912 presidential election. In the 1920 elections, he received nearly a million votes while in prison, convicted in 1918 of a crime of opinion. Debs opposed the U.S. entry into the First World War, for which he was sentenced to ten years under the Sedition Act and pardoned by President Warren G. Harding three years later due to the cardiovascular problems he developed in prison. That in fact. Following our formula, we see that Debs is pardoned when the Socialist Party had been dismantled and the First World War had been resolved with the defeat and humiliation of Germany and the consolidation of the Paris-London-Washington axis.

Until a few years earlier, the harsh anti-imperialist criticisms of writers and activists like Mark Twain were demonized, but there was no need to tarnish the reputation of a free society by imprisoning a recognized intellectual, as they had done in 1846 with David Thoreau for his criticism of the aggression and dispossession of Mexico to expand slavery, under the perfect excuse of not paying taxes. Neither Twain nor the majority of public critics managed to change any policies or reverse any imperialist aggression in the West, as they were read by a minority outside the economic and financial power. In that aspect, modern propaganda had no competition, so direct censorship of those critics would have hindered their efforts to sell aggressions in the name of freedom and democracy. On the contrary, the critics served to support that idea, by which the greatest and most brutal empires of the Modern Era were proud democracies, not discredited dictatorships. The Free World, the Civilized World...

All ideological and narrative fossils, like when people repeat "extremes are bad." This popular maxim is easy to understand in medicine; even drinking too much water is dangerous. It also seems easy to understand when talking about political issues. It is assumed that we are in the center and that any call for radical change is extremism. Nothing new. During slavery, abolitionists were demonized as extremists,

$P - d.t = 0$

proponents of the end of civilization, the divine order of God, and the freedom and prosperity of societies.

Today, saying that a tiny minority has taken control of countries and is leading the planet to catastrophe is considered extremism.

FREEDOM OF SPEECH IN OPEN SOCIETIES

THROUGHOUT THE LAST four centuries of humanity, the most brutal, racist, oppressive, and genocidal empires have been democracies. Political democracies and economic dictatorships. Liberal regimes framed by a single ideology, capitalism, and justified by multiple strategic fictions turned into dogmas, such as the Free Market and Human Rights. At the same time, major private companies since the early 17th century, such as the East India Company, the West India Company, or the Virginia Company, were plundering and massacring millions of people from Asia to America, instilling racism and racial and hereditary slavery; at the same time as they imposed the worst forms of colonialism known in history, destroying prosperous societies through drugs, cannon fire, and protectionist tariffs; at the same time as they destroyed free markets, their propaganda machinery sold their own discourse about "the free market," the "expansion of civilization," the "promotion of freedom and democracy," "the struggle for justice," and the unique recipe for "the progress and prosperity of peoples."

In fact, there was also another notable paradox. Those same brutal global dictatorships and, even national dictatorships, such as in the case of the slave-owning United States, allowed (by law and, not infrequently, in practice) the freedom of expression of their own citizens and even of foreigners. The ethnic dictatorship of the United States (1776-1868) enacted and protected from the beginning the right to freedom of expression and conscience in its First Amendment. This freedom, like the earlier "We the people" (1787), did not include Blacks, Native Americans, or Mexicans, despite "all men are created equal" (1776). When the Confederacy of the South went to war to destroy the Union (United States) and thus maintain the "Peculiar Institution" (the slave system, it established in its 1861 constitution the sacred right to private property (especially of other human beings) while explicitly establishing the right to "freedom of speech," albeit somewhat more limited than the original Union's: "Congress shall make no law respecting an establishment of religion, or prohibiting the free exercise thereof; or abridging the freedom of speech, or of the press; or the right of the people peaceably to assemble, and to petition the Government for a redress of grievances. A well-regulated Militia being necessary to the security of a free State, the right of the people to keep and bear Arms shall not be infringed." That is, freedom of speech as long as slavery and the power of slaveholders were not questioned.

In fact, there was also a notable paradox. Those same brutal dictatorships and, even national dictatorships, such as in the case of the slave-owning United States, in fact allowed the freedom of expression of their own citizens and, not infrequently, of foreigners. This freedom of expression to criticize the dominant power was, from many perspectives, undeniable and unquestionable. Even Karl Marx, exiled from the Prussian regime, found refuge in England where, from his poverty, he wrote scathing critiques of British colonialism and, thanks to the translations from German to English by his friend Frederick Engels, was able to publish them in the New-York Daily Tribune.[1] Both managed to survive in England with some money sent by Engels' father and the ten cents per article paid by the New York newspaper. Both lived under the surveillance of the British police, but censorship did not prevent them from publishing articles in newspapers, nor even the first and most critical historical analysis of the capitalist system, *Das Kapital,* a few years later. The first volume of *Capital:*

A *Critique of Political Economy* was published in 1867 and the last in 1894. Karl Marx only saw the publication of the first volume.

Eight years after the publication of the third volume of *Capital*, in 1902, the British professor John A. Hobson published *Imperialism: A Study*, where he criticized the brutality of the empire of which he was a citizen and dismantled the meritocratic logic of the superior race: "Britain has become a nation living on foreign tribute, and the social classes that enjoy this tribute have an ever-greater incentive to use public policy, public funds, and public force to expand the field of their private investments and thus safeguard and improve their private investments."[II] Hobson was marginalized by critics, discredited by academia and the mainstream press of the time. He was neither arrested nor imprisoned. While the empire he himself denounced continued to kill millions of human beings in Asia and Africa, neither the government nor the British Crown took the trouble to directly censor the economist. Not a few, as happens today, pointed to him as an example of the virtues of British democracy. Something similar to what happens today with those critics of American imperialism, especially if they live in the United States: "look, he criticizes the country he lives in; if he lived in Cuba he wouldn't be able to criticize the government." In other words, if someone points out the crimes against humanity in the numerous imperial wars and does so in the country that allows freedom of expression, that is proof of the democratic virtues of the country that massacres millions of people and tolerates someone daring to mention it.

For Hobson, the highest stage of capitalism was imperialism, the nationalist enterprise of a financial system dominated by an oligarchy at the heart of the Empire, which exploited not only the colonies but also the workers of the imperial nation. This idea (along with Marx's principle of capital accumulation) would be taken up by Lenin in his 1916 analysis Imperialism, the Highest Stage of Capitalism.

Examples of dissent within the northwestern empires are numerous and notable. How is it possible that Great Britain, France, and the United States, the two centers of the capitalist and Anglo-Saxon hegemonic power, would allow this radical type of freedom of expression within their own core?

Every paradox is an apparent contradiction with an internal logic. In *Flies in the Web* (2023) we summarize it as follows: "*An imperial power, dominant, unchallenged, without fear of the real loss of its privileges, does not need direct censorship. In fact, the acceptance of*

$$P - d.t = 0$$

marginal criticism would prove its virtues. It is tolerated, as long as they do not cross the line of true questioning. As long as hegemonic dominance is not in decline and in danger of being replaced by something else".

SLAVEHOLDERS CARE ABOUT FREEDOM OF EXPRESSION

JAMES PHELPS, UPON HIS RETURN FROM TEXAS on January 16, 1825, writes to Stephen Austin from Mississippi: "There is no other reason that holds back the wealthy plantation owners of Louisiana from investing in Texas more than the issue of slavery. *We have read with concern in the press that the Republic of Mexico has approved some laws that prohibit the introduction of blacks* as private property without any exception, threatening those who violate these laws with the most humiliating measures. We are also informed that this republic has decided to emancipate all the slaves now owned by the colonists of Texas, as well as any other black slave who sets foot on Mexican territory."

Also, a letter from the wealthy cotton planter Charles Douglas arrives, dated February 15, 1825, from Alabama, expressing concern about the Mexican government's obstinacy against slavery (which would not encourage the arrival of the wealthiest cotton growers, he assures) and its questionable commitment to the tolerance of different religions and "freedom of conscience." Four years later, from Veracruz, on April 25, 1829, the same Douglas will write again reflecting on the difference between the freedom of whites and the licentiousness of blacks, between the good governance of the slave states and the mismanagement of the countries of the South: "our most valuable inhabitants are the blacks, and no American owner is willing to move to Mexico unless they are first guaranteed the right to property."

On July 24, the Texan Juan Seguín, future hero of the Texas War of Independence and later expelled from his own land for being Mexican, writes to Stephen Austin: "Friend, I understand that you cannot convince your countrymen to emigrate to Texas if we do not allow them to bring their slaves. But that argument is not even heard in our national congress."

The officials of that barbaric country discover that the immigrants receive Mexican lands and impose their own laws. The slaves increase in number every day. At first, the authorities merely notify the fact. They insist: in this land, it is illegal to own slaves. The immigrants continue with their business, and the warnings become annoying. On June 4, Randall Jones writes to Austin prophetic words: "This province must be populated as quickly as possible so that, at a certain moment, the majority manages to impose slavery." Meanwhile, the immigrants from the North send letters promising to obey the laws of Mexico, but once on the other side, they forget their promises. The laws of the country that welcomes them and gifts them land are absurd, unjust, contrary to nature and property.

Fifteen years later, in 1840, Colonel Edward Stiff will publish his memoirs *The Texan Emigrant*, in which he will acknowledge that "*we are so proud of our work and demand the right to kidnap and enslave others for life, especially those who have a different color, so that they can be distinguished from us and remain subjected to slavery by their appearance; we want blacks* and only a blind man cannot see that we do not care how we treat them; as good citizens and as descendants of those who hate the mere presence of a black man as much as that of a Catholic priest, we take the liberty to declare that if we are not allowed to enslave those children of Africa, descendants of Cain, their children, and their children's children, and if, in addition, we are not allowed the right to pray to the Creator according to our tender freedom of conscience, we will have at least two good excuses to rebel."

DISSENT, DIVERSITY, FREEDOM OF EXPRESSION

ON JANUARY 1, 1831, *The Liberator* appeared in Massachusetts, the country's first abolitionist newspaper and, later, a defender of women's suffrage. At the time, the slaveholders of Georgia offered a reward of $5,000 (over $160,000 at 2023 value) for the capture of its founder, William Lloyd Garrison. Naturally, this is how power reacts to freedom and the struggle for the rights of others, but this attempt at violent censorship was not then the legal norm. The freedom of speech established by the First Amendment applied to white men and no one wanted to break the law in broad daylight. To correct these errors, there were always the mafia, paramilitarism, and later, secret agencies that operated beyond the law—or legal harassment under other pretexts.

In its first article, Garrison already revealed the tone of a dispute that promised to be long-lasting: "*I am aware that many object to the severity of my language; but is there not cause for it? I will be as harsh as truth and as uncompromising as justice*. On this subject, I do not wish to think, speak, or write with moderation. No! Tell a man whose house is on fire to give a moderate alarm, to moderately rescue his wife from the hands of the rapist, to gradually save his child from the fire…"[III]

The Liberator, exercising its right to freedom of the press, began sending copies to the southern states. The response of the southern governments and slaveholders was not to ban the publication, as it was against the law—a law that was made for some white and wealthy men to protect themselves from other white and wealthy men who never imagined that this freedom could threaten the political power of all white and wealthy men in any way.

Instead of breaking the law, they resorted to an old method. It is not necessary to break the rules when you can change them. This is how democracy works. Of course, not everyone had, nor has, the same opportunities to perform such a democratic miracle. Those who cannot change the laws often break them, and that is why they are criminals. Those who can change them are the ones most interested in ensuring they are followed. Except when the urgency of their own interests does not tolerate bureaucratic delay, or when, for some reason, an inconvenient majority has

been established, which those in power accuse of being irresponsible, childish, or dangerous.

Initially, since they could not directly abolish the
First Amendment, they limited the losses. North Car-
olina passed laws prohibiting the literacy of slaves.[1]
The prohibitions continued and spread throughout
the 1830s to other slave states, almost always justified
by the disorders, protests, and even violent disturb-
ances that abolitionists had instigated among Black
people with subversive literature.

Pro-slavery propaganda did not take long to appear, and posters and pamphlets were distributed
warning of *subversive elements* among the decent people of the South and the dangers of the few lectures
on the taboo subject. The harassment of freedom of
speech, without reaching outright prohibition, also
occurred in the major cities of the North. One of the
pro-slavery pamphlets, dated February 27, 1837 (a

---

[1] The laws did not explicitly prohibit slaves from learning to
read and write. They prohibited those who knew how to do so
from teaching slaves to read and write. Similarly, today there
are no laws that prohibit anyone's education; in fact, the opposite is true. But various policies make education inaccessible to
those who, for example, cannot afford it, while at the same
time stimulating the commerce of entertainment, distraction,
in other words, the opposite of education.

year after Texas was taken from Mexico to reestablish slavery), invited the population to gather in front of a church on Cannon Street in New York, where an abolitionist was scheduled to speak at seven in the evening. The announcement called to "silence this diabolical and fanatical instrument; let us defend the rights of the States and the constitution of the country."[IV]

Publications and abolitionist lectures did not stop. For a time, the way to counter them was not through the prohibition of freedom of speech but rather through an increase in pro-slavery propaganda and the demonization of anti-slavery advocates as dangerous subversives. Later, when propaganda was no longer enough, all the Southern states began to adopt laws that limited the freedom of speech regarding revisionist ideas. Only when freedom of speech (freedom of white dissenters) spiraled out of control did they resort to more aggressive laws, this time limiting freedom of speech with selective prohibitions or taxes on abolitionists. For example, in 1837, Missouri banned publications that went against the dominant discourse, that is, against slavery. It was rare to resort to the disgrace of imprisoning dissenters. They were discredited, censored, or lynched under some good pretext such as self-defense or the defense of God, civilization and liberty.

After the Civil War broke out, the slaveholding South wrote its own constitution. Just as the Anglo-Saxon Texans had done after separating from Mexico and for the same reasons, the Constitution of the Confederacy established the protection of the "Peculiar Institution" (slavery) while including a clause in favor of freedom of expression. This clause did not prevent laws that limited it on one side or the paramilitarism of the slave militias (origin of the Southern police) from acting at will. Like the "We the people" in the 1789 Constitution, and like the original First Amendment of 1791, this "freedom of expression" did not include people who were neither "the people" nor fully human and responsible beings. It referred to the free race. In fact, the constitution of the new slaveholding country stated, in its section 12, almost as a copy of the original 1791 amendment: "Congress shall make no law respecting an establishment of religion, or prohibiting the free exercise thereof; or abridging the freedom of speech, or of the press; or the right of the people peaceably to assemble, and to petition the Government for a redress ofgrievances."[V] More fair, equitable, and democratic, impossible... The secret was that, once again, as almost a century before, this "the people" did not include the majority of the population. If anyone had pointed this out at the time, they would have been called crazy, unpatriotic, or a dangerous subversive. In other words, something that, at its core, has not changed much in the 21st century.[2]

By the time the slave system was legally abolished in 1865, thanks to the circumstances of a war that was nearly lost, The Liberator had already published 1820 issues. In addition to supporting the abolitionist cause, it also supported the movement for equal rights for women. The first female candidate for the presidency (though not legally recognized), Victoria Woodhull, was arrested days before the 1872 election on charges of having published an article deemed obscene—opinions against public morality, such as women's right to decide over their sexuality. As has

---

[2] This interpretation was seared into place by the very constitution of 1861, which, while consolidating the right to slavery, sought to eradicate the bad example of "free Blacks" who could be introduced from the North and who were largely *exported* to Haiti and Africa, where they founded Liberia. Section 9 stated: *"The importation of Blacks of African descent from any foreign country other than the slaveholding States or Territories of the United States* of America is prohibited; Congress is required to pass laws that effectively prevent this possibility."

been the norm for centuries in the free world, Wood-hull was not arrested for exercising her freedom of expression in a free country, but under the pretext of violating other laws.

However, this is not an exclusive characteristic of the slaveholding South or of the United States as a whole. The British Empire always proceeded in the same way, not much different from "Athenian democracy" twenty-five centuries ago: "We are civilized because we tolerate different opinions and protect diversity and freedom of expression." Of course, as long as certain boundaries were not crossed. As long as they did not become a real threat to our unchallenge-able power.

In this sense, let us remember only one example to avoid making this book a voluminously impossible and unpublishable experience. In 1902, the economist John Atkinson Hobson published his now-classic *Imperialism: A Study* where he explained the vampiric nature of Great Britain over its colonies. Hobson was marginalized by critics, discredited by academia and the mainstream press of the time. He was not arrested or imprisoned. While the empire he himself denounced continued to kill millions of human beings in Asia and Africa, neither the government nor the British Crown bothered to censor the economist directly. Not a few, as happens today, pointed to him as an example of the virtues of British democracy. Something similar to what happens today with those critical of American imperialism, especially if they live in the United States: "Look, they criticize the country they live in; if they lived in Cuba, they wouldn't be able to criticize the government." In other words, if someone points out the crimes against humanity in the multiple imperial wars and does so in the country that allows freedom of speech, that is proof of the democratic virtues of the country that massacres millions of people and tolerates someone daring to mention it.

How can all these apparent contradictions be explained? It's not that complicated. An imperial, dominant power, without opposition, without fear of truly losing its privileges, doesn't need direct censorship. In fact, the acceptance of marginal criticism would prove its virtues. It is tolerated, as long as they don't cross the line of true questioning. As long as the hegemonic dominance is not in decay and in danger of being replaced by something else.

Now let's look at those counterexamples of hegemonic power and its stewards. Why don't you move to Cuba, where people don't have freedom of speech, where there is no plurality of political parties?

To begin with, it would be necessary to point out that all political systems are exclusive. In Cuba, they don't allow liberal parties to participate in their elections, which are dismissed as a farce by liberal democracies. In countries with liberal democracy systems, like the United States, the elections are basically elections of a single party called Democratic-Republican. There is no possibility that a third party could seriously challenge the One Party because it is the party of the corporations, which are the elite that holds the real power in the country. On the other hand, if, for example, in a country like Chile, a Marxist like the current president Gabriel Boric wins the elections, it doesn't even occur to anyone to imagine that this president will step outside the constitutional framework, which prohibits the establishment of a communist system in the country. The same happens in Cuba, but it must be said that it's not the same.

Now, let's return to the logic of freedom of expression in different global power systems. To sum it up, I think it's necessary to say that freedom of expression is a luxury that, historically, those colonies or republics fighting for independence from the empires could not afford. It would suffice to recall the example of Guatemalan democracy, destroyed by the Great Democracy of the United States in 1954 because its democratically elected government decided to apply the sovereign laws of its own country, which did not suit the megacorporation United Fruit Company. The Great Democracy did not hesitate to install another dictatorship, one that left hundreds of thousands dead over decades.

What was the main problem of Guatemalan democracy in the 1950s? It was its freedom of the press, its freedom of expression. Because of this, the Northern empire and the UFCo managed to manipulate public opinion in that country through a propaganda campaign deliberately planned and acknowledged by its own perpetrators—not by their native overseers, needless to say.

When this happened, the young Argentine doctor, Ernesto Guevara, was in Guatemala and had to flee into exile in Mexico, where he met other exiles, the Cubans Fidel and Raúl Castro. When the Cuban Revolution triumphed, Ernesto Guevara, by then known as El Che, famously summarized: "Cuba will not be another Guatemala." What did he mean by this? Cuba would not allow itself to be manipulated like Guatemala through "free press". History proved him right: When in 1961 Washington invaded Cuba based on the CIA's plan that claimed "Cuba will be another Guatemala," it failed spectacularly. Why?

Because its population did not join the "liberation invasion," as it could not be manipulated by the massive propaganda that "free press" allows. Kennedy knew this and reprimanded the CIA, which threatened to dissolve and ultimately did.

Freedom of expression is characteristic of systems that cannot be threatened by it, but rather the opposite: when popular opinion has been crystallized, either through tradition or massive propaganda, the majority's opinion is the best form of legitimization. This is why these systems, always dominant, always imperial, do not grant their colonies the same rights they afford their own citizens.

When the United States was in its infancy and fighting for its survival, its government did not hesitate to pass a law prohibiting any criticism of the government under the pretext of spreading false ideas and information—just seven years after enacting the famous First Amendment, which did not stem from religious tradition but from anti-religious European enlightenment. Naturally, that 1798 law was called the Sedition Act.

These resources of the champion of free speech were repeated multiple times throughout its history, always when the decisions and interests of a government controlled by the corporations of the day felt seriously threatened. This was the case with another law also called the Sedition Act, the one from 1918, when there was popular resistance against propaganda organized by figures like Edward Bernays in favor of intervening in World War I—thus ensuring the collection of European debts. Until a few years earlier, the harsh anti-imperialist criticisms of writers and activists like Mark Twain had been demonized, but there was no need to tarnish the reputation of a free society by imprisoning a renowned intellectual, as they had done in 1846 with David Thoreau for his criticism of the aggression and dispossession of Mexico to expand slavery, under the perfect excuse of not paying taxes. Neither Twain nor the majority of public critics managed to change any policies or reverse any imperialist aggression in the West, as they were read by a minority outside economic and financial power. In that regard, modern propaganda had no competition, so direct censorship of these critics would have hindered their efforts to sell aggression in the name of freedom and demo-cracy. On the contrary, critics served to support this idea, by which the largest and most brutal empires of the Modern Era were proud democracies, not discredited dictatorships.

Only when public opinion began to waver too much, as during the Cold War, did McCarthyism emerge with its direct persecutions, and later the (indirect) assassination of civil rights leaders and violent repression, with prisoners and deaths on campuses, when criticism of the Vietnam War threatened to translate into effective political change—indeed, the Congress of the 70s was the most progressive in history, enabling the Pike-Church Committee to investigate the CIA's regime of assassinations and propaganda. When two decades later the invasions of Afghanistan and Iraq took place, public criticism and demonstrations had become inconsequential and self-satisfying, but the new magnitude of imperial aggression since 2001 made it necessary to enact new legal measures, as in 1798.

History rhymed again in 2003, except that instead of the *Sedition Act* it was called the Patriot Act, and it not only established direct censorship but something far worse: the indirect and often invisible censorship of self-censorship. More recently, when criticism of racism, patriotic history, and the excessive rights of sexual minorities began to expand beyond what was controllable, the recourse to legal prohibition returned. Such is the case with the latest laws in Florida, promoted by Governor Ron DeSantis, directly banning revisionist books and regulating language in public schools and universities—just for starters. The creation of a demon called Woke to replace the loss of the previous demon called Muslims.

Meanwhile, the stewards, especially the colonial lackeys, continue repeating clichés created generations ago: "How is it that you live in the United States *and criticize that country? You should move to Cuba, where freedom of expression is not respected*." After their clichés, they feel so happy and patriotic that it's a shame to disturb them with reality.

On May 5, 2023, the coronation ceremony of King Charles III of England took place. Journalist Julian Assange, imprisoned for over a decade for the crime of having published a minor part of the atrocities committed by Washington in Iraq, wrote a letter to the new king inviting him to visit the depressing Belmarsh Prison in London, where hundreds of prisoners languish, some of whom were recognized dissidents. Assange was granted the sacred right to freedom of expression generously bestowed by the Free World. His letter was published by various Western media, proving the virtues of the West and the childish contradictions of those who criticize the Free World from within the Free World. But Assange continues to serve as an example of lynching. Even during slavery, a few Black men were publicly lynched. The idea was to set an example of what could happen in a truly free society, not to destroy the same oppressive order by eliminating all the slaves.

POWER AND FALSE DISSENT

ONE OF THE NATURAL MANIFESTATIONS of any power fossilized at the apex of the social pyramid is the division of those below. The capitalist variation of this ancient law, *divide et impera*, lies in the explicit inoculation of racism and the demobilization, disarticulation, and demoralization of any social organization that is not the guild of millionaires—those who can call for capital strikes whenever they please (in the name of the sacred right to private property of their capital) and pressure the people with necessity and hunger every time they decide to do the same: unite to defend their individual rights, their class interests, their dignity as colonized peoples.

The massive protest movement of American students against the massacre in Gaza, which significantly ignited the spark for other uprisings in other Western countries, appears as a *paradoxical phenomenon*. At least this is how journalists who have consulted me on the matter have expressed it.

Like all paradoxes, it is a logic that seems contradictory: in the country where its citizens are known for their geopolitical ignorance, for their disinterest, if not insensitivity, toward their own imperialist wars and their blind patriotism, for their addiction to consumption and their militaristic and religious fanaticism, the student protests belong to a tradition that began in the 1960s with anti-war movements, continued in the 1980s with their protests against apartheid in South Africa, and later with various demands for divestment from their powerful universities' involvement in the war business, private prisons, and ecocidal pollution.

As in all cases, attempts were made to discredit them as irresponsible and dreamy young people, when it was precisely these youths who were the most informed and the bravest of their society, despite not coming from a group submerged by the violence of basic needs. This is also not hard to explain: it is not only the non-commercialized knowledge, nor the less corrupted idealism of the youth that accounts for this reaction, but also the fact that no one can imagine a union of *homeless* organizing to demand better living conditions, not because they are productive but simply because they are human beings.

But I believe there is another reason that explains this phenomenon and it is probably one of the main reasons. As I noted at the beginning, the division of the lower classes has always been a weapon of domination for those at the top. I could dwell on a multitude of crucial examples from the last two centuries, but the rule is so basic that few would question it. One of its translations, demobilization, was and remains an unwritten but entrenched policy within the capitalist system itself: first, demobilization through the dismantling and demonization of social organizations, such as workers' unions. Second, through the comfort of churches that, in their vast majority, supported or justified economic, political, and social power. Third, through the only sacred secularization that was allowed: consumerism and the dogma of individualism. Selfishness and greed, for centuries two sins among the Christian communards of the first three centuries of existence in illegality, and moral sins in most of the social philosophies of antiquity, in the 16th century became sacred virtues to please and support the fever of the new capitalist ideology.

But let us return to the specific case of American students. Anyone who has been a student or professor in the United States has a clear idea of how campus life operates. Although some come from the upper classes and do not need scholarships or loans because their parents pay for their education in full, the vast majority borrow money from their own future to pay the most expensive tuition in the world. Others, with more luck or initial merit, receive scholarships. In any case, without class distinction despite being inserted into a fiercely segregationist national and global system, where privileges and class struggle are no less fierce, on campuses these differences are attenuated to the point of almost disappearing. That is the first point.

The second point, equally contradictory to the rest of social reality, lies in the permanent social, group, almost familial interaction of university students. A large part (sometimes a large majority) lives in campus apartments. Those who do not, it is as if they lived there. In my classes, for example, barely ten percent come from the city where the university is located, despite Jacksonville having a million inhabitants. Most come from states as far away as New York or California and from continents as diverse as Europe, Latin America, Africa, and Asia. I would be surprised if next semester I do not have a class with this pattern. This wonderful diversity (sure, the poor are a minority, but they exist thanks to scholarships) produces a human and global consciousness that is not seen in the provincial fanaticism of much of the rest of society and that is better known in the rest of the world, because the ridiculous and absurd tends to popularize and go viral more quickly.

The third point (for these reflections it is the first) lies in the fact that this way of life not only exposes young people to different thoughts in their classes but also to different ways of life in living with their foreign classmates, from sports distraction and park barbecues to some excessive parties in their fraternities and sororities with their extreme jokes—one day I arrived at my office as the sun began to rise and, on the way, I encountered underwear and bras hanging from a tree that preceded the entrance to a building where I usually teach. Youthful antics.

As a professor, I have been a member of various committees, such as the student committee, and although my critique of the American university system lies in its lack of democracy compared to Europe or Latin America because, for example, students do not vote, they still manage to organize and demand claims they consider just and necessary.

In other words, students are not misinformed, demobilized, disorganized, and frightened as they will be when they become a cog in the machine. This makes them *dangerous* to the system, which explains their powerful protests on 50 campuses across the country for a human rights cause they considered just, necessary, and urgent.

The example of students with no power other than their own unity deserves to be taken seriously. The first to understand this was the political (economic and media) power, which is why they not only allowed violence against the students but also repressed them with irrational violence, detaining 3,000 of them and none of the fascists who initiated the violence in the cappings.

A corollary to this is the urgent need for the rest of society to reorganize into groups and unions again, not just workers' unions, but all kinds of unions, from grassroots political committees to neighborhood committees. This can be achieved using the very instruments of division and demobilization that have been used against them: digital technology.

We will have a new world when individuals join different groups, different assemblies, even if virtual, to discuss, to listen, to propose, to feel a sense of belonging to something beyond the poor individuality of consumption. If humans are selfish, we are no less altruistic. When we identify a just cause, we fight for it beyond our own interests. There are plenty of examples.

Will we come to understand again that the common interest of humanity, of the species, is, at least in the long term, the most important interest of the individual? In the recovery of this communal sense, of this involvement, lies the salvation of the individual and of humanity.

Over time, this multiplicity of communities at different levels and with different interests will ensure that voluntary donations and imposed taxes stop flowing to the ultra-wealthy who buy presidents, senators, armies, and even global opinion. Because the rich do not donate, they invest. When they don't invest in politicians, judges, and journalists, they invest in the market of morality. As a rule, not an exception, the rich always have a personal motivation for donating.

Humans are driven by self-interest and by a collective cause. There's no need to clarify which, in political and ideological terms, is the right and which is the left. In any case, both interests are human and must be considered in the equation that will make this anxious, violent, and unsatisfied species something better. For that, the majority must cease to be a disposable, irrelevant class.

WORKERS ARE DANGEROUS TO FREEDOM

IN CHICAGO, THE WORKERS who since February 1886 refused to have more of their salary deducted to build a church doubled down and demanded a law to protect the right to an eight-hour workday. Like wildfire, two hundred thousand workers initiated a massive strike in demand for the three eights that make up a 24-hour day: eight hours to sleep, eight to work, and eight to live as human beings.

Three days later, the peaceful protests ended with the Haymarket massacre and, ultimately, in the death sentence of the workers who were not on the side of the strongest. Eight union leaders were accused of anarchism, and five of them would pay with their lives. The tragedy was one of many and the culmination of years of labor struggles and persistent demonization by the major press in service of the big investors.

As usual, a few decades later, a powerful businessman from the upper class hijacked the old demands of the lower class. Henrry Ford banned all unions in his micro republics and boasted of having invented

$$P - d.t = 0$$

the benefit of the eight-hour workday. The racist genius, admirer and collaborator of Hitler, had calcu-
lated that if the wage earners of the country did not
have some free time to consume, no one could buy
his products.

In memory of the massacre and executions in Chicago, the first of May is a non-working holiday in almost the entire world, except in the United States
and, by extension, in Canada. For the nationalist fanatics, believers in the divine right of the owners of
the world, the two words (international and workers)
sound very dangerous. The recent political defeat of
the Confederation in favor of slavery was offset by several cultural and ideological victories. All went unno-
ticed. One of them consisted of idealizing the masters
and demonizing the slaves. That is why, for many
generations to come, the United States will celebrate
Memorial Day (in memory of those who fell in wars)
and Veterans Day (in honor of the veterans of those
endless wars). One is an abstract title; the other, something all too concrete. For the workers, there has
never been, and still is not, a Workers' Day, much less
a May Day. To forget about this inconvenience, President Cleveland officially established Labor Day in
September, almost the opposite of May, as if there
could be work without workers, which signifies a

hidden triumph of the slaveholders defeated in the Civil War: the blacks, the poor, the downtrodden, the workers, are not only lazy, inferior, and, as future president Theodore Roosevelt would say, "perfectly idiotic," but also perfectly dangerous. Above all, because of their numbers, just as, they said, the blacks were. Above all, because of that habit of proposing unions. The masters (white), the upper class, the champagne-sipping elites, are the ones who create jobs with their investments. They are the ones who, from time to time, must be protected by the churches and by the military (in the United States with the cult of the war veteran who "protects our freedom" and in Latin America the military that corrects the mistakes of democracy with bloody dictatorships or with eternal threats). For the old slaveholding tradition, for the masters of what the wind carried away but always returns, the true makers of progress, stability, peace, and civilization are the plantation owners, the industrial entrepreneurs. They are the elite of the chosen people and represent everything that the dirty, foul-mouthed slaves (later white wage workers from poor Europe; later mestizos from the sick and corrupt South) always want to destroy.

Of course, there is no complete power without powerful allies, like the dominant press, like the compliant churches. On May 17, 1886, like so many other prestigious newspapers from different states, the *St. Louis Globe-Democrat* from Missouri, on its fifth page and across seven wide columns, expounded on the conflict of workers who do not want to work more than eight hours a day:

"In this dispute, the only impartial institution is the church, supported by capitalists and workers, as it was founded by Christ, a carpenter, and therefore has every right to speak for all workers; the church owns the planet Earth, the Solar System, and the entire Universe, which also allows it to speak for the capitalists."

THE TROTSKY OF THE BRONX

IN 1916, THE RUSSIAN SHIP ASKOLD docked in the port of Marseille. Shortly after, a mutiny on board resulted in the murder of an officer, forcing French authorities to intervene. During the inspection, several copies of the Russian newspaper Nashe Slovo (Our Word) were found, published by Trotsky and considered anti-Russian literature by the regime of Nicholas II. Interrogated by the French authorities, Trotsky claimed that the copies had been planted by Russian officers.

In October, without explanation, the French authorities entered his apartment at 31 Rue Pompe in Paris and took him away, leaving his wife, Natalya, and their two children to their own devices. The detainee was suspected of being against the war. They took him to the Spanish border and dumped him on the other side, in the Basque Country. In San Sebastián, he was arrested, again without legal reason, and taken to Madrid, where a few days later, after a visit to the Prado Museum, he was imprisoned and then transferred to Cádiz for shipment to Cuba.

For Trotsky, there was no doubt: the Spanish authorities were responding to the orders of the French authorities, who were responding to the orders of the Russian authorities, who were responding to the orders of the French banks that had already invested heavily in the dictatorship of Nicholas II. In prison, he began to study English, awaiting the efforts of his friends (among Spanish republicans and American socialists) who saw no other solution to his life in exile than the New World. Finally, the efforts paid off, and the authorities approved his trip to the United States.

In the usual interrogation before boarding, he replied that he was neither an anarchist, nor a polygamist, nor an alcoholic, nor mentally retarded, and that he had never lived in a poorhouse. These were necessary conditions, apart from being white, for the immigration authorities of the time. He even lied when he said he had never been imprisoned. Trotsky had been imprisoned many times in Tsarist Russia, for his writing, for organizing workers' unions, and for organizing the protest against the massacre of a thousand demonstrators in St. Petersburg in 1905.

Natalya also lied to the immigration officer: she had been imprisoned for participating in a workers' meeting in St. Petersburg to commemorate May Day and the massacre of workers in Chicago. At that time, the brutal dictatorship of Tsar Nicholas II (Emperor of Russia, King of Poland, and Duke of Finland) had not only persecuted all kinds of dissidents but had also left nearly half a million dead in the famine of 1891-92. Nicholas II, a renowned nationalist and anti-Semite like his predecessors, would have been Hitler's main ally had he not been dethroned by the October Revolution—or the November Revolution, depending on the calendar used. It was probably this historical factor that contradicted Karl Marx's prediction: it would not be an industrialized society that would see the proletariat take power, but rather an agricultural and medieval society, like Russia's. Nicholas II's father had executed Lenin's older brother by hanging, and the October Revolution, led by Lenin, executed Nicholas II. A century later, the Tsar and his family would be canonized by the Russian Orthodox Church as holy martyrs.

Trotsky had adopted that name from his jailer in Siberia in 1902, but in 1917 he managed to travel to New York under his original surname, Bronstein. After a 17-day journey, the steamer announced its arrival in New York at 3:00 a.m. It stopped at Ellis Island, a mandatory stop where, under the gaze of the Statue of Liberty, immigrants had to prove that they were healthy, that they did not indulge in alcohol, and, if possible, that they were white. If they were traveling first class, they didn't even have to go down to the island because the officers would board their cabins. This was the case with the Trotsky family. Aside from Immigration, the family was welcomed by several editors and members of the Socialist Party. Party lawyer and Marxist theorist Louis Boudin took them to dinner.

Meanwhile, Lenin continued his exile in newspapers from his own exile in Switzerland. Trotsky had separated from Lenin in 1902 for ideological and personal reasons. According to Trotsky, Lenin was a "terrible egocentric." According to Lenin, Trotsky was a "Judas," an "evasive cheat." For Lenin, there could be no proletarian revolution without a revolutionary vanguard and a centralized state that would lead a profound reform of society before ascending to higher levels of social justice. Trotsky, less pragmatic, was closer to the anarchists, rejecting a vertical structure in favor of grassroots popular organizations, such as trade unions and popular assemblies—the soviets. For Trotsky, Lenin's idea of a "dictatorship of the proletariat and peasants" was more of a "dictatorship over the proletariat and peasants."

The idea or principle that united them was simple: wars are products of national bourgeoisies (just as in the Middle Ages they were products of the nobility, not the peasants, the pawns in the chess game) and are promoted by nationalism, as they had previously been by another unifying element: religion. At that time, many socialists and anarchists understood that the union of the world's workers would negate the main cause of the greatest injustices and tragedies in the world, where workers and their children marched to kill other workers in the name of a nation and for the benefit of the ruling classes. The First World War was merely a confirmation of this thesis: the workers of some countries united against the workers of their neighboring countries thanks to a nationalist fanaticism that brought them no benefit but death, destruction, and poverty.

In 1917, New York was still a kind of anarchist republic. Newspapers and books were published in dozens of languages, from Spanish to Russian. The plays were performed with actors from various countries and for different communities. Novy Mir (New World), a weekly newspaper published in Russian in a modest workshop at 77 Saint Marks Place in Staten Island, was both Bolshevik and Menshevik. Lenin used to read Novy Mir in his exile in Switzerland, so he learned of Trotsky's reception in America. "Had I been the King of England, I would not have been treated better," Trotsky commented.

Various newspapers announced his arrival in New York aboard the Monserrat. The Trotsky family had been expelled from Russia, Austria, Germany, France, and finally, Spain at the request of the Russian diplomatic network, and the newspapers used this anecdotal information as their headline. "Expelled from Four Countries," headlined the New York Times on its second page on January 15. For his anti-war and anti-nationalist preaching, the country's largest newspaper described him as a socialist, Marxist, and "Russian pacifist," who had arrived with his wife and two sons, Leon, 11, and Serge, 9. On the same page, the New York Times reported a purge of progressives from the Tsar's Russian government, replaced by supporters of the extreme right. The Yiddish-language socialist newspaper, The Jewish Daily Forward, with a circulation of over 200,000 copies per day, featured Trotsky on the front page of Tuesday, January 16.

Trotsky stayed for two months in an apartment on Wise Avenue in the Bronx. On November 4, after he had returned to Russia, The Baltimore Sun described Trotsky as an anarcho-socialist and the second most important figure of the Russian Revolution, after

Lenin. A few months later, in September, the Bronx Home News headlined: "A Bronx Man Leads the Russian Revolution."

In New York, the tertulias were a refuge for socialists and anarchists expelled from Europe and, often, tried and convicted in America. For some reason, the racist right-wing of the Ku Klux Klan and the powerful businessmen of the time (a few years later, Nazis and fascists; a few decades later, neoliberals; a century later, libertarians) were rare birds in these cultured circles. Race, country, and money were always bastions of the right. Culture and non-commercial thought were not. Hence their traditional obsession with demonizing or eliminating the arts, humanities, sciences, and nonprofit universities.

Theodore Roosevelt believed that (foreign) anarchists were taking over the country, or he wanted this theory to be widely believed as a classic electoral strategy, so he ordered close surveillance of anyone suspected of being an anarchist. In 1908, the Bureau of Investigation was created with the hidden purpose of being an ideological police force rather than a federal criminal investigation force. In 1924, Edgar Hoover became director of the Bureau of Investigation, which nine years later would become the FBI. Hoover would not relinquish his position or his obsession with pursuing all types of individuals with ideas or sentiments outside of national dogma (socialists and lesbians alike) until his death in 1972, almost half a century later.

In New York, Trotsky discovered his popularity across the Atlantic. The socialist newspaper published in German since 1878, the New Yorker Volkszeitung, recorded Trotsky's remarks such as: "I am a stateless person and I am glad to have found a country that has accepted me within its borders." In fact, he was surprised to find an open political and intellectual environment, uncensored and unpersecuted. In other words, the antipodes of what the United States would become a few decades later, colonized by religious fanaticism and the Protestant obsession with faith, which would translate into McCarthyism in the 1950s and all kinds of ideological persecution by the media, Edgar Hoover's FBI, Allen W. Dulles's CIA, and others, perfect representatives of the United States' ideological police.

The Russian Revolution did not do much differently with freedom of the press. The same Trotsky who had recognized this type of freedom in New York, a few months later became the second most important leader of the new USSR, after Lenin. He was

Foreign Minister of a government that banned not only conservative but even socialist newspapers.

There will always be excuses for limiting freedom of expression, but history shows that it is a luxury of dominant regimes, those against which criticism has no chance of effective change, as was the case with the British and American empires, as evidenced by their constitutional protection even during slavery and anti-imperialist criticism within these empires, such as John Hobson in England and Mark Twain in the United States, to name just two.

WORKERS STEAL FROM INVESTORS

IN 1919, IN THE SUPREME COURT of justice in Michigan, an event occurred with ideological consequences that have now surpassed a hundred years, though its roots lie in 16th-century England, as we will explain in an upcoming book, something to read with less urgency and anxiety—at least that is the superstition of every writer who wastes their life researching things that interest few and benefit even fewer.

A paradoxical protagonist and victim was Henry Ford, one of the many millionaire admirers and decorated individuals of Hitler, with an aristocratic and racist sense of societies. Seven years later, his decision to grant his workers one of the rights most long sought by unions in the West, the eight-hour day (8-8-8, eight hours for work, eight for rest, and eight for living), was based on the idea that workers should have time and purchasing power to expand the businesses of those above them. Like Hitler, Ford had also set out to produce a *people's car* (*Volkswagen*) that could carry a man at the wheel, his wife by his side, and three children in the back.

By the second decade of the 20th century, and due to the success of the *Fort T* that still rolls along the streets of the old Portuguese city of Colonia del Sacramento in Uruguay, Ford Company had accumulated an excess of capital, which led its manager, Henry Ford, to decide to increase his workers' wages. To a large extent, it was a publicity strategy and, above all, Ford's suspicion that some shareholders were accumulating profits to open their own company and compete with his (like the Dodges, who were already supplying mechanical parts to Ford itself), but in practice, it was going to benefit the company's workers.

Shortly after learning about Henry Ford's plans to let some profits trickle down to his workers, brothers John and Horace Dodge, who owned ten percent of the company's shares, sued Ford Co., arguing that the accumulated capital belonged to the shareholders, not the workers, whose wages were already competitive in the market. What more was needed? The lawsuit was based on the accusation that the workers were stealing money that rightfully belonged to the investors.

In 1919, the Michigan Supreme Court sided with the Dodge brothers, which not only allowed them to receive extra capital to start their own *Dodge Motor Company* and produce millions of friendly cars that invaded the rest of the world as proof of the benefits of capitalism, but—more importantly—it set a legal, cultural, and ideological precedent. Since then, rulings by other courts and other outlets turned into written dogma the idea that *capital and its profits belong to the shareholders, not the workers*.

Explicitly, the state Supreme Court ruled that company managers must operate their companies for the benefit of their shareholders, not for the charity of their workers. This philosophy closely resembles that of the slave system, abolished half a century earlier, but still thriving in the rest of the dominant culture, replicated and practiced from media mogul William Hearst to every CEO of the most powerful transnational corporations in the country.

Needless to say, the same obvious truths were adopted and defended as the lifeblood of the colonies in the Global South—and little has changed since then.

In the hegemonic center, ideological dissent began to shrink until there was no longer any doubt: the rich are the ones who create jobs. Just as slaves in chains had to thank their masters for their daily meals, now wage workers had to thank those who decided the fate of millions of people from a yacht with a glass of whiskey in hand. It was clear who should reap almost all the benefits of the economic system: those who not only "took more risks."

FROM HERO TO VILLAIN

On May 26, 1933, the celebrated General Smedley Darlington Butler delivered a speech on war and imperialism in Arlington, Virginia. From that day on, he began a journey that would take him from the pedestal of a national hero to the corner reserved for the poor madmen. Few, stated the general, know what they are talking about when they speak, as they ignore that the true purpose of imperialism and its wars is motivated by "the benefit of a few at the expense of the masses."

Butler proposed limiting military force to the protection of borders so that it could truly be called defense, and then continued: "The problem is that when the dollar benefits us only at six percent, we go to other countries and take one hundred percent. In this way, the flag follows the dollar, and the soldiers follow the flag. I would not go to war again to protect the investments of bankers... Our wars have been very well planned by nationalist capitalism. I served in the Navy for 33 years, rising to the rank of General, and during that time, I spent most of my time being the muscle of Wall Street and big business... In short, I was a mafioso of capitalism... I never had time to stop and think until I retired from service. Like any military man, my mind was suspended and occupied with following orders... In 1914, I worked to ensure the interests of American oil companies were secure in Mexico. I did the same in Haiti and in Cuba to ensure the National City Bank had a decent place to operate freely in pursuit of profits. I participated and collaborated in the rape of the republics of Central America for the benefit of Wall Street. From 1909 to 1912, I helped 'clean up' Nicaragua so that the Brown Brothers bank could continue profiting from that country, even though I didn't even know it existed before arriving. I did the same in the Dominican Republic in 1916, protecting the interests of our sugar companies. The same in China, so that Standard Oil could be free from any limitations. When I look back, I think I could give Al Capone a few lessons, with the difference that he operates in three districts and I operated on three continents."

People leave the conference in shock, and General Butler feels he needs to explain a bit more. In 1935, he will publish a book titled *The Racket of War*, but it will also not be well received by critics. As in his previous conferences, the general donates his fees to the unemployed, which, apparently, is strong evidence that the former national hero has an ideology.

That same year, before a congressional committee, Butler will testify that he had been chosen by a group of billionaires to lead a coup against the socialist president Franklin Roosevelt. If he refused, the second candidate would be General Douglas MacArthur, the third General Hugh Samuel Johnson, and fourth Handson MacNider. MacArthur, critical of Roosevelt's new policies, is against pacifism and in favor of increasing military power, but the president proposes to cut its budget in half. The public dispute between the two figures will end with the general vomiting in shame as he leaves the White House. TIME magazine chooses General Hugh Johnson as "Man of the Year" instead of the recently elected president, but the following year Roosevelt will remove him from the National Recovery team due to his sympathies with Italian fascism. As for MacNider, he is a recognized general and a politician repeatedly frustrated at the polls. The plot, according to General Butler's testimony, funded by J.P. Morgan among other powerful financial groups, aims to remove the socialist president from the White House.

Franklin Delano Roosevelt is also accused of being a socialist by his political opponents, such as the

Democratic governor of New York, Al Smith. His policies of subsidies for the poor, the creation of Social Security (which had already existed in Uruguay and some European countries), the New Deal with labor unions, and his bet on the State as the driver of economic recovery through public works earn him the hatred of conservatives and capitalists. The old party of Andrew Jackson and James Polk, the conservative party of pro-slavery Southerners, swaps places with the liberal Republicans of the North. From then on, the Democrats become the American left, largely supported by the inhabitants of the industrialized North, and the Republican Party of Lincoln becomes the conservative arm of the Southern states.

General Smedley Butler, after participating in almost all the wars his country intervened in across Central America, the Caribbean, Asia, and Europe over the last two decades, had become a national hero and the most decorated military officer of his time. Retired in 1931, he ran for the Senate the following year but lost by a wide margin. By then, Butler was already facing resistance from a portion of the press due to his uncomfortable comments and his numerous conferences, through which he raised scandalous sums of money that he donated to the unemployed. The press mocked his allegations of a supposed coup

d'état in Washington and preferred to repeat his criticism of Benito Mussolini and the "nascent fascism in
the United States." He also included his criticism of
President Roosevelt, whom Butler had accused of
bending to the weight of the super-rich elite. Foreign
Service magazine published some of his scandalous
statements, such as: "We must grab Wall Street by the
neck and shake it."

After two months of investigation, a House of
Representatives committee, led by Congressmen
John W. McCormack of Massachusetts and Samuel
Dickstein of New York, confirmed the existence of
the plot with *"alarming clarity"*. However, what glit-
ters blinds. Although no evidence will ever be pro-
vided, the committee will be accused of being funded
by the Soviets, and in 1938 it will become something
very different: the House Un-American Activities
Committee, tasked with pursuing anyone suspected
of communism. Due to their popularity at the time,
Nazis were excluded from any suspicion.

On November 22, 1934, on its page 20, the *New
York Times* will label the decorated general's accusation and the House committee's conclusions as a
"massive fiction."

Case closed.

THE FREE WORLD DURING THE COLD WAR

IT WAS ONLY WHEN PUBLIC OPINION began to waver too much, as during the Cold War, that McCarthyism emerged from the depths of hegemonic power (P). The Soviet Union had not only defeated the greatest military power of the time, Nazi Germany, nearly single-handedly, but it also continued to present an alternative example of economic and social success, despite its questionable gulags and Stalinist censorship. It was the alternative that, in just four decades, had turned a rural and impoverished country into an industrial power that had increased life expectancy by several years—something similar to what communist and Mao Tse-Tung's adversary China would achieve after the catastrophe of the Great Famine of 1958-1962 and, even more spectacularly, starting in the 1980s with its new reforms. To make matters worse, by the late 1950s, the USSR had won the space race by launching the first satellite, the first living creature (the dog Laika), and the first human into orbit.

With its direct persecutions and later the (indirect) assassination of civil rights leaders and the violent repression with arrests and deaths on university campuses during the criticism against the Vietnam War threatened to translate into effective political change—in fact, the 1970s Congress was the most progressive in history, making possible the Pike-Church Committee investigation against the CIA's regime of assassinations and propaganda. When two decades later the invasions of Afghanistan and Iraq took place, criticism and public demonstrations had become insignificant and self-complacent, but the new magnitude of imperial aggression starting in 2001 required new legal measures, as in 1798.

Now, let's return to the logic of freedom of expression in different global power systems. To summarize, I believe it is necessary to consider that freedom of expression is a luxury that, historically, those colonies or republics fighting for independence from imperial freedoms could not afford. It would suffice to recall the example of Guatemalan democracy, destroyed by the Great Democracy of the United States in 1954 because its democratically elected government decided to apply the sovereign laws of its own country, which did not suit the megacorporation United Fruit Company. The Great Democracy did not hesitate to install another dictatorship, one that left hundreds of thousands dead over decades. The same story in Iran, Chile, Congo, Indonesia, Burkina Faso… Just limiting ourselves to the Cold War.

What was the *main problem* of Guatemala's democracy in the 1950s? It was its freedom of the press, its freedom of expression. Through this, the Northern empire and the UFCo managed to manipulate public opinion in that country through a deliberately planned propaganda campaign, acknowledged by its own perpetrators—not by their local lackeys, it goes without saying.

When this happened, the young Argentine doctor, Ernesto Guevara, was in Guatemala and had to flee into exile in Mexico, where he met with other exiles, the Cubans Fidel and Raúl Castro. When the Cuban Revolution triumphed, Ernesto Guevara, by then known as Che, summarized it remarkably: "Cuba will not be another Guatemala." What did he mean by this? Cuba would not allow itself to be inoculated like Guatemala through the "free press." History proved him right: When in 1961 Washington invaded Cuba based on the CIA's plan, which assured that "Cuba will be another Guatemala," it failed spectacularly. Why? Because its population did not join the "liberating invasion," as they could not be inoculated by the

$P - d.t = 0$

massive propaganda that the "free press" allows. Kennedy knew this and reprimanded the CIA, which threatened to dissolve and ultimately was dissolved.

PUBLIC OPINION AS A
CONSUMER PRODUCT

ON AUGUST 15, 1953 THE PRESIDENT Dwight Eisenhower signed the authorization for Operation PBSuccess, with which the CIA had resolved to overthrow the president of Guatemala, Jacobo Árbenz, by inventing the story of the communist threat. In the words of Theodore Roosevelt's grandson, Kermit Roosevelt Jr, who a year earlier had successfully participated in the overthrow of another democratically elected president, Mohamed Mossadegh, "Guatemala will be another Iran." In Guatemala, only four of the 61 elected congressmen were communists, and their influence in the army, as in any other Latin American army, was zero. Not without irony, it is the communists who advise the president on the option of a capitalist reform, that is, that the lands to be expropriated do not pass to the government but to the private hands of Guatemalan farmers.

On December 3, 1953, the CIA approves a budget of three million dollars for this operation, to which it

will later add another four and a half million.3 In support, John Foster Dulles appoints John Peurifoy as
ambassador to Guatemala, a failed West Point student who wanted to be president of the United States
and who, with that goal, had secured the position of
elevator operator at the Capitol through a special favor from a well-known congressman. Dulles senses
that the former elevator operator has what he needs:
a reliable paranoia about "the red danger." In December, shortly after the arrival of the new ambassador
Peurifoy, the deputy chief of the U.S. embassy in Guatemala and surviving diplomat, William L. Krieg,
completes his report and states that the reactionary
and oligarchic forces are "first-rate vagabonds... para-
sites who only think about money," while the communists "worked hard, have ideas, and are aware of
the purpose of their work," in addition to being "honest and committed." The tragedy, adds Bill Krieg, is
that "the only people who are committed to hard
work are those who, by definition, are our enemies."

By the twists of fate, almost all those involved in
planning the coup against Árbenz are investors in the
United Fruit Company: the Secretary of State, John

---

3 In total, 75 million dollars at 2024 value.

Foster Dulles; the director of the CIA, Allen Dulles; the Assistant Secretary of State for Inter-American Affairs and brother of the former director of United Fruit Company, John Moors Cabot; the senator and ambassador to the UN, Henry Cabot Lodge; the secretary of President Eisenhower, Ann Whitman, wife of Edmund Whitman, CIA press director; Walter Bedell Smith, Undersecretary of State, who will be part of the board of directors of the United Fruit Company.

The economic reasons are deep and extensive but easy to understand. In 1936, the current Secretary of State, John Foster Dulles, as a lawyer for the firm Sullivan & Cromwell, had matured the banana monopoly of the United Fruit Company for Guatemala, all with the invaluable assistance and support of the dictator of the time, General Jorge Ubico.4 Since then, John had also been the representative of Railways of Central America and Electric Bond & Share. Now, together with his brother, the CIA director Allen

---

4 American companies had dominated the politics and economy of the region since the last century. By the mid-20th century, Samuel Zemurray, founder of Cuyamel Fruit Company, the mastermind behind the coup in Honduras in 1911 and later director of UFCo, had recognized that "in Honduras, a legislator is worth less than a mule."

Dulles, he leverages the powerful apparatus of the world's greatest superpower to prevent the poor in some remote part of the world from obtaining a small piece of land in their own country to produce basic food and threatening the authority of the successful in the North. The UFCo's party in Guatemala had ended in 1944 when the philosophy professor Juan José Arévalo and his "Spiritual Socialism" inspired by Franklin Roosevelt won the country's first free elections. With the unknown democracy began a rare period of reforms that limited the land gifts and tax exemptions that benefited The Octopus during the dictatorship of Jorge Ubico. Resorting to his classic method of making others say what he wanted the people to repeat, just as he had previously placed a cigarette in the mouths of opera singers, the mercenary propagandist Edward Bernays places a banana in the hands of Hollywood stars and begins the makeover of The Octopus. As always, Bernays' propaganda campaign is a complete success.

It's not just about reducing production costs through subsidies and starvation wages. The ideology of business requires a psychology and an ethics at its service. The almost absolute dependence of workers on companies like UFCo prevented the poor from retiring to their own lands, ceasing to be wage earners and desperate consumers. Long before its massacres in Latin America, UFCo knew it had to inoculate the desire for material things in its southern wage earners. This was not a new idea, not at all. A century earlier, to decree the abolition of traditional slavery in its Caribbean possessions, the British had designed a type of slavery desired by the new slaves. On June 10, 1833, a member of Parliament, Rigby Watson, had put it very clearly: "To make them work and create in them a taste for luxuries and comforts, they must first be taught, little by little, to desire those objects which can be attained through labor. There is a progression from the possession of necessities to the desire for luxuries; once these luxuries are attained, they become necessities in all social classes. This is the type of progress through which the blacks must pass, and this is the type of education to which they must be subjected."

UFCo took note and put it into practice. In 1929, its most promoted journalist (and friend of Henry Ford), Samuel Crowther, reported that in Central America, "people only work when they are forced to. They are not accustomed to it, because the land provides them with the little they need... But the desire for material things is something that must be cultivated... Our advertising has the same effect as in the

United States and is reaching the common people, because when a magazine is discarded here, people pick them up and their advertising pages appear as decoration on the walls of thatched huts. I have seen the interiors of the huts completely covered with pages from American magazines... All this is having its effect in arousing the desire for consumption in people."

Samuel Crowther considered the Caribbean to be the lake of the American Empire, which protected and directed the destiny of its countries for the glory and development of all.

But development does not come; on the contrary. Nor does the desire for the consumption of material goods come with the same force as the desire for freedom and democracy that is sweeping Latin America, and by this point, has already toppled several dictatorships. With the election of Jacobo Árbenz, a captain from the upper class but with that tendency some have of looking downward, the reforms of Professor Arévalo continued without becoming radicalized. During his government, hundreds of committees of poor peasants had been formed to discuss and administer the new lands, which at the time was seen as an unmistakable sign of communism or something equally dangerous. When Árbenz assumed the presidency, 70 percent of the population was illiterate, a figure that rose to 90 percent among the indigenous population, meaning more than 60 percent of Guatemalans were subjected to forced labor with no remuneration by tradition and a life expectancy of 38 years. Between the UFCo and the Creole oligarchy, 2 percent of the population owned 72 percent of the land in a country whose economy was almost exclusively based on agriculture.

The tension and conflict of interests created by the democratic period of 1944-1954 claimed the lives of two landowners, but this was not enough to stop the process of democratization in the country. In 1950, Árbenz had begun a land reform plan that affected 1.3 percent of the land available for agriculture. The reform included the expropriation of a smaller fraction of unproductive lands held by the UFCo, lands that the company had received from the dictatorships before Arévalo.[5] The Octopus did not accept being

---

[5] The government had proposed nationalizing 95,000 hectares given away by the dictator Jorge Ubico to UFCo, just twice the area of the ranch owned by U.S. President Lyndon Johnson in Chihuahua in the 1970s, against Mexican law and the constitution.

paid the value it had itself declared in its taxes ($2.98 per acre) and demanded the sum of $75 per acre.

With the democratic president overthrown and replaced by General Castillo Armas, one of the many puppets who are never hard to find, Edward Bernays, the CIA, and the Eisenhower administration will continue the effort to clean up the image of the nervous little dictator. Before the successful coup, the mustachioed general with a Hitler-style mustache was already known to Washington. In 1946, he had completed a training course at Fort Leavenworth, Kansas, and in 1950, he had failed in his attempted coup against Arévalo. In 1953, the CIA had located him in Honduras and brought him to a training session in Opa-Locka, Florida. They then paid him $3,000 a month (equivalent to $29,000 in 2020) plus provisions for his 140 men. Every action Castillo Armas and his men participated in ended in defeat and with several dead. The CIA never cared because this group was not operational; it merely represented the second main excuse to keep the press occupied.

Now Vice President Richard Nixon will invite him to Washington to speak on television about the communist government of Árbenz, overthrown by the Guatemalan people who never accepted the lie and foreign intervention (the backdrop will show a cross as the spear of Saint George over the hammer and sickle). The nervous general tells Nixon, "Tell me what you want me to do, and I'll do it immediately." In the years and decades to come, the successive dictatorships of Guatemala will not be able to hide the hundreds of thousands massacred as a result of Washington's savior schemes. Just one of these, the dictator Efraín Ríos Montt, will order the massacre of 18,000 indigenous people in 1982. Shortly afterward, during his visit to the tropical hell, President Ronald Reagan will praise the genocidaire as an example of the fight for freedom in Guatemala and against the "regime" of their Nicaraguan Sandinista neighbors. The most powerful churches in the United States, such as the Club700, will also support their evangelical brother until his death in 2018.

Despite the brutal campaign, the CIA acknowledges that, both in Guatemala and in Latin America, the communists are a minor force. The Agency and some Latin American armies, such as the Argentine one, will make the same diagnosis before embarking on the adventure of saving their countries with more coups. In 1954, out of the 61 Guatemalan legislators, only four are communists. Except in the workers' unions, where, for obvious reasons, they have some prominence. As it has been for a century, the central problem is not communism but disobedience that is conveniently labeled as communism. Before Árbenz was elected president, the U.S. embassy had sent a list to President Juan José Arévalo with names that needed to be removed from his government, but the president, in an unusual attitude, had ignored the request. Threatening the benefits of a U.S. company under the guise of a law passed by some banana congress was another clear demonstration of insubordination. Even the CIA History Department researcher, Professor Nicholas Cullather, will conclude decades later that the United Fruit Company often reported profits and values much lower than the actual ones to evade taxes, but Edward Bernays convinced the U.S. Congress and public opinion otherwise: "it wasn't about bananas, it was about communism." From the start, the idea was very convincing. "Wherever you see criticism or discussion of the United Fruit Company, you should substitute the company's name with that of the country, the United States States." Some reports describe Jacobo Árbenz as a conservative politician. The U.S. military in Guatemala also sees no "communist danger," but, as in the invasion of Mexico 110 years earlier, they act against their own opinions in the name of efficiency, duty, and honor. Until decades later, some of them have a conscience crisis and begin to speak their minds.

At this point, Edward Bernays is the advisor to the company in question (the United Fruit Company), the most important propagandist of the century and the inventor of modern Public Relations. He personally selects the journalists he considers the least informed from the Times, Newsweek, The New York Times, and the Chicago Tribune and sends them to Guatemala with everything paid for by the United Fruit Company to "report on communist activities" in Central America. During the trip to Guatemala, amid cigars and plenty of whiskey, the organizers ensure the dogma is crystallized among the journalists: they were all covering the events of a country that had been taken over by a Marxist dictatorship. The Russians prefer vodka. Once inoculated, upon arriving in the actual country, the reporters' vision aligns with the dogma, not reality, and quickly translates into headlines in the U.S. press and the Public Opinion of the Free Country.

The only journalist who dares to mention the reasonable land reform of President Jacobo Árbenz and the population's dissatisfaction with the U.S. transnational corporation is Sydney Gruson of The New York Times. Shortly after, the business director of The

New York Times receives a visit from his friend, the director of the CIA, Allen Dulles, and Sydney Gruson will be removed from the Central America beat.

Without ever setting foot in Guatemala, Bernays knows what it's all about. That's his job: not just to know what others ignore but to make them believe what his clients want others to believe. Bernays is an old mercenary, and he's so good that his annual salary (one hundred thousand dollars, not counting bonuses) is higher than that of any U.S. president. The nephew of Sigmund Freud, his interest is not so much the study of the human mind but the money derived from its manipulation. In 1924, he had convinced President Calvin Coolidge to cook pancakes for his followers during his re-election campaign, a populist tradition that would survive as a dogma into the 21st century. In 1927, with his "Torches of Freedom" campaign, he had managed to get women to start smoking to increase the profits of Lucky Strike cigarettes. Even unsuspecting feminists fell into his trap. The great Bernays is also responsible for Americans eating eggs with bacon, which he achieved to increase the sales of his client, the Beech-Nut Packing Company of New York. He is also one of the masterminds behind the sale of wars and coups, such as this one in Guatemala. Not only had Adolf Hitler read with admiration the book The Passing of the Great Race (The Defeat of the Superior Race) by the American Madison Grant, to whom he wrote thanking him for providing him with his political bible, but also his future propaganda minister, Joseph Goebbels, had Edward Bernays' books in an accessible place in his library (yes, Goebbels also had Jewish friends). In the 1940s, Bernays had been hired by the United Fruit Company, known for its tentacles as The Octopus, a multinational that had ruled over the Caribbean and Central America since the 19th century with budgets larger than any of the banana republics in which it operated freely.

Now, the strategy is clear: it is necessary to shake the ghost of communism once again. There are ample means, and none are disregarded. It is very easy to be a genius when there is plenty of money. The powerful CIA agent Howard Hunt Jr. visits the Catholic bishops of the United States and convinces them about the danger of Guatemala, so the bishops are quick to condemn the communism of President Árbenz. On April 9, 1954, a pastoral letter reaches the hands of Archbishop Mariano Rossell y Arellano and then, other more elaborate ones, to the bishops of Guatemala warning of the dangerous forces "enemies of God and the Homeland." Rossell y Arellano will be decisive in the destruction of democracy and the rule of law in his country and will leave his post as archbishop, as often happens, when he dies in 1964. Shortly before the coup d'état, on April 4, 1954, he will commission a wooden Jesus, later reproduced in bronze, who will be baptized as the Christ of Esquipulas. Thus, Jesus, who in life detested weapons as much as he favored the poor and marginalized, will be used as "Commander-in-Chief" of the fascist forces of the National Liberation Movement against the government of Árbenaz and in favor of the American empire, without considering that Jesus was executed by the empire of the time as a mere criminal, alongside two others and for political, not religious, reasons. The archbishop's statement reads: "We raise our voices to alert Catholics that the worst atheist doctrine of all time (anti-Christian communism) continues its shameless advance in our country, disguising itself as a social reform movement for the most needy classes... Every Catholic must fight communism by their very condition as a Catholic... They are people without a nation, scum of the earth, who have repaid the generous hospitality of Guatemala by preaching class hatred with the aim of plundering and destroying our country completely." The talking points work perfectly in Spanish. Catholic fanaticism closely re-sembles its old enemy, Protestant fanaticism.

Less powerful, the main unions of Guatemala still support the president. Even if Árbenaz were not a communist, even if, as in any country in Latin America, the communists were a very small minority, convincing people in the United States and in Guatemala that he was, poses no problem.[6] The right of other peoples to be whatever they choose to be, even communists, is not even on the table. Without the slightest proof, radios and major newspapers begin publishing the Washington narrative: "We are convinced of the ties between Guatemala and Moscow." More than enough. After all, a country with an ultra-secret agency like the CIA always knows more than the rest of mortals and reserves the right to provide evidence "for security reasons."

------

[6] As in most Latin American countries of the time, the Soviet Union did not have an embassy, and its presence was, compared to the omnipresent (both legal and illegal, governmental and private) presence of the United States, insignificant and irrelevant. Like Patrice Lumumba in Congo and other Third World leaders who were cornered by the foreign policies of Europe and the United States, Árbenz would turn to Czechoslovak aid, when it was already too late.

At the OAS, the representative of Guatemala, Guillermo Toriello Garrido, protests against the organization's resolution on the right of other nations to intervene if the influence of communism is confirmed. The resolution is presented at the behest of the CIA director, Allen Dulles, who at the same Caracas meeting praises the Venezuelan dictatorship of Marcos Pérez Jiménez as exemplary. Amid the international noise, Toriello could see clearly what millions cannot and will not: "it is very distressing that any nationalist or independent movement must be labeled as such [communist], as well as any anti-imperialist or anti-monopoly action... And the most critical thing of all is that those who label democracy in such a way do so in order to destroy that very democracy."

Mexico, Argentina, and Uruguay are the only ones supporting Toriello's arguments, criticizing all types of interventionism, and opposing the "Caracas Declaration." But they abstain from voting, and Guatemala is left alone. The resolution 93 pushed by Washington is forceful and proposes "to adopt the necessary measures to protect the political independence [of American countries] against the intervention of international communism, which acts in the interests of foreign despotism, and reiterates the faith of the people of America in the effective exercise of representative democracy." The political literature of power, known as Realism or Realpolitik, is endowed with infinite freedom of patriotic imagination.

Meanwhile, in Opa-Locka, Florida, the fictitious campaign of Radio Liberación continues preparing public opinion for the final stage, while pretending to be a rebel radio station operating from the Guatemalan jungle. As a complement, and as it will be a long tradition in the continent, the CIA and the USIA plant, by force of dollars, at least 200 articles in various Latin American newspapers denouncing the communist danger in Guatemala.[7] It is only part of the plan. Although the U.S. officials consider Árbenz's policies "democratic and conservative," Guatemala does not even secure loans from the World Bank to carry out its agrarian reform. Some Guatemalan landowners are furious and request assistance from the Nicaraguan dictator Anastasio Somoza, who during his visit to President Truman at the

---

[7] Planting opinion pieces in major Latin American media outlets would not be the only recurring practice of the CIA. Another custom, which would be uncovered by researchers many decades later, included the introduction of weapons into friendly or enemy groups to be discovered by the unsuspecting local press.

White House in April last year had informed him, in his good English: "Just send me the weapons, and I will clean up Guatemala for you in one fell swoop."

Since Árbenz's victory in the 1950 elections, Washington has refrained from selling arms to the new government. A terrible sacrifice, but for a good cause. In 1953, it blocked the purchase of defensive materials from Canada and Germany, but now it delivers the best weapons to the Guatemalan exile in Honduras and Nicaragua. On February 9, in collaboration with the FBI, the CIA finalizes its Operation Washtub, through which it plants Soviet weapons on the coast of Nicaragua to be discovered by fishermen and the dictatorship of Somoza can accuse Guatemala of communist plans in the region.

With no other options, President Arbenz (as Patrice Lumumba would do in Congo seven years later) would turn to Czechoslovakia. On May 5, 1954, the Scandinavian ship MS Alfhem would arrive at Puerto Barrios with a shipment of weapons that would prove obsolete, providing a new excuse for Washington's intervention. In June, the CIA would bomb the British ship Springfjord with Napalm in Puerto San José, which turned out to be a shipment of cotton and coffee from the American company Grace Line, making it one of the few mistakes for which the CIA would be sued. On May 27, 1954, the friendly dictator Anastasio Somoza informed the press that, besides the weapons found, there were photographs of the Soviet submarine that had transported them, bound for Guatemala.

In 1987, Major John R. Stockwell, a CIA officer involved in the operation, would admit that "the killing of 85,000 Guatemalans by governments supported by the United States has not made new friends for this country, I can assure you... In the end, the United Fruit Company went bankrupt and its chairman committed suicide". Another CIA agent, an active member of the operation in Guatemala, Navy Colonel Philip Clay Roettinger, was in charge of training soldiers in Honduras and bringing General Castillo Armas, "that nervous little man", to the presidency. In 1986, Roettinger would admit that "no one in the government thought Guatemala could pose any threat to the United States... the only threat the Guatemalan government could represent was to the interests of the United Fruit Company; that was the only reason". Years after the coup, Roettinger would leave it all behind and move to Guanajuato, Mexico.[8]

---

[8] According to CIA archives in a "Declassified Copy" from 2011 of an article dated March 16, 1986, Colonel Roettinger would

Things did not go well for the new dictator, General Castillo Armas either. Before being assassinated in 1957, the mustached general in the style of Hitler was honored by Columbia University with an honorary doctorate for his "struggle for democracy" (a reason why Rómulo Gallego would return his degree conferred by the same institution). Castillo Armas visited Washington and appeared on a television program with Vice President Richard Nixon. With a backdrop of a hammer and sickle crossed by the relentless spear of the cross, Nixon would say: "The case of Guatemala *was a rebellion of the people against a communist regime… in other words, the regime of Jacobo Arbenz* was not a government of Guatemala but one controlled by foreign forces". The general and supreme dictator of Guatemala, Castillo Armas, responded to everything with "yes, yes". He did not

---

write that Árbenz was more capitalist than socialist, a president who intended to transform dependent capitalism into a "modern capitalist state," meaning too independent. In "For a CIA Man, It's 1954 Again" Roettinger would lament, "our success led to 31 years of military dictatorship and 100,000 people killed, aside from destroying the necessary economic and social reforms in that country… now President Ronald Reagan *tells us the same thing that the CIA director at the time, Allan Dulles,* told us in Florida, that our fight is against communism…"

understand English, nor did he understand anything else. He only knew that his repressive force came from members of Jorge Ubico's regime (an unapologetic Nazi in a country of indigenous people), that his regime had banned the Russian writer Fyodor Dostoevsky as subversive, and that a few years ago someone had told him that, perhaps, the United States could help him become president after losing the elections to the damned Jacobo Arbenz.

On December 29, 1996, the UN would sponsor a Peace Agreement in Guatemala. By then, two percent of the population would own half of the arable land in Guatemala. 200,000 people would have been killed under successive military dictatorships, 93 percent of them executed or massacred by the Soldiers of the Fatherland. In 1999, President Bill Clinton would visit the country and acknowledge his country's responsibility for the destruction of democracy in 1954 and the subsequent support for genocidal military regimes. "The support of the United States to the Guatemalan army and the intelligence involved in the violence in Guatemala was a mistake that should never be repeated," he says. The same tears will fall in 2010 when the Secretary of State, Hillary Clinton, acknowledges the atrocity committed by Washington by conducting experiments with syphilis and gonorrhea on the poor of Guatemala in the forties. As always, everything happens when it no longer matters to anyone or has any consequences for the victims. Nor for power.

Or almost.

THE PRICE OF PRESS FREEDOM

In 1976, the United States Senate published the final report of the Church Commission investigations on abuses by the National Security Agency and the CIA, from planning coups and assassinations of foreign leaders to tracking domestic dissenters and the planned introduction of ideological propaganda in the realms of culture, academia, media, news agencies, unions, and religious groups. Any group or organization with some social prestige has been infiltrated with the purpose of creating public opinion for or against something or someone or, simply, to prevent something or someone from gaining any social relevance and sinking into obscurity and ostracism. When in 1963 the CIA knew before anyone else that Pablo Neruda was a strong candidate for the Nobel Prize in Literature in 1964, they immediately began a smear campaign, infiltrating the media and targeting leftist readers with the rumor that in 1940 Leon Trotsky had been assassinated, with the

P - d.t = ▯

complicity of the Chilean poet.[9] Neruda, García Márquez, Eduardo Galeano and many others were on
Washington's list of banned visitors, but like the others, in 1966 Neruda had managed to tour the United
States, not only due to the demands of Arthur Miller
and other American intellectuals but because it did
not suit the government's image to make public the
ban on names respected in so many countries. The
CIA and the FBI kept close tabs on him, always in
search of some compromising detail, like Martin Luther King's fondness for women and John Lennon's
never-discovered weakness. When the Guatemalan
Nobel laureate Miguel Ángel Asturias (another fierce
critic of the Vietnam War and American imperialism
was proposed for the presidency of the PEN of New
York, the CIA pressured Miller to take the position.
This time they succeeded, but the failures of their suc-
cesses will accumulate in the long run.

---

[9] The rumor was based on the visa that the then-consul Neruda
granted to the painter to travel to Chile, when Siqueiros was in
jail for the possible failed conspiracy of May 24th, three months
before Trotsky's assassination in his studio at the back of Diego
Rivera and Frida Kahlo's house in Coyoacán, Mexico. Finally,
the Nobel Prize will not be awarded to Neruda that year but to
another communist and, like Neruda, a critic of the Vietnam
War, Jean Paul Sartre.

The CIA and other indirect foundations invested mountains of dollars, as no other organization on the planet could, and used Washington's powerful intelligence network to promote "art for art's sake" and neutralize the Latin American wave of the "committed author," but once realizing that the wave was bigger than the surfer, especially because the endless coups sponsored by Washington had ended up promoting their rebel authors, there was a change in strategy. They resorted to negotiation where one party cedes some ground to include their adversary in their own territory. That is, the CIA itself, with its own agents and spies, like Howard Hunt, and through its satellite foundations, like the Congress for Cultural Freedom, began publishing Neruda himself and García Márquez in cultural media that mostly went against the radical ideas of these writers. Those involved in these cultural manipulations, like Howard Hunt, don't call it propaganda or ideology but "defense of the country" and "propagation of American values."

Now, a couple of years after the Watergate scandal that led to President Nixon's resignation, a minor part of these secret activities is being revealed in Washington. From now on, conspiracies and manipulations will be more airtight and sophisticated.

Based on current laws and rights, Frederick Schwarz Jr., assistant to Senator Frank Church of Idaho who heads this commission, requests more information from the NSA and its director, who, considering its area of action is not the United States, responds that "the Constitution does not apply to the NSA." Though labeled as Final, it is a report and a fifteen-month investigation that falls short by several leagues. Although courageous in its context, it does not fail to reveal the problems of its culture and the dominant ideology (spread by the CIA's propaganda services in coordination with the leading newspapers of Latin America) when it considers that President Salvador Allende's international relations with some socialist or communist country could be mitigating factors for foreign intervention.

The scandal, which will be silenced by other noises and quickly forgotten by a sufficient majority of the population, had begun less than two years earlier when, on December 22, 1974, on its front page, the *New York Times* had published leaked information that, for some time, attempts were made to deny by resorting to the accusation of "conspiracy theory." The newspaper had accused the Nixon administration of using the CIA to harass American dissidents protesting against the Vietnam War and other pacifist movements. The CIA, the article claimed, had created at least ten thousand files on peaceful citizens suspected of not being true Americans or not patriotic enough.

In his questioning of several agents, Senator Frank Church had accused the CIA of paying journalists, writers, academics, and hundreds of other media outlets to spread propaganda around the world. The CIA does not agree to provide a list of names, but the powerful agent Howard Hunt, with extensive experience in Latin America, does not deny any of the accusations.10 On the contrary, he confirms and justifies them as "acts of patriotism." One of the most common practices consists of funding in different countries the translation or publication in their original language of thousands of aligned books, especially by "repentant communists" or "non-committed" writers, functional to Washington's cause. Another resource, according to agent Hunt and administrator for a time of the millions of dollars allocated to this

---

[10] Some, like the remorseful agent Philip Agee in his memoirs Inside the Company: CIA Diary, directly mention various Latin American newspapers that published editorials written by CIA employees, sometimes from the United States, and habitual articles with false information.

type of culture, was to amplify the reach of reviews by recognized critics who were favorable to the books promoted by the Agency or, otherwise, to obtain negative reviews of undesired books.

In the United States, the project for extensive ideological intervention in the press had been established long before, in 1948, by the National Security Council, later known as Operation Mockingbird, in honor of the bird that mimics the songs of others. In Latin America, it took the Nahuatl name of Sinsonte, the bird of four hundred songs, through which the CIA planted editorials and fictional news in the most important newspapers of the continent, especially when it was about to perpetuate an invasion, a coup d'état, or simply needed a favorable vote in the OAS. Sometimes this creation of public opinion was carried out through hundreds of paid scribes, by temporary mercenaries, or by facilitating with secret information the work of writers and journalists who worked honorarily, with greater conviction and some need to promote their careers. In other cases, it was preceded by the necessary cultivation of the friendship of the owners of the main media who frequented expensive parties and gatherings where a CIA or Embassy agent fulfilling his Public Relations work was never missing. Agustín Edwards Eastman, owner of

El Mercurio in Chile and instigator of the coup against Allende in Santiago and at the White House, is just one of the most well-known cases that also includes owners or directors of radio stations, television channels, magazines, and any medium that shapes public opinion.[11]

Although it is the most strict, disciplined, and powerful intelligence agency in the world, the CIA had numerous failures and no few fiascos. But it was always extremely creative, and its ideas never lacked the support of millions of dollars from Washington. When it was deployed to Uruguay in 1957, its agents often used huge tape recorders that were received through diplomatic mail, which would break down every week, and after some time, they would throw them into the bay of Montevideo to avoid raising suspicions. As head of CIA operations in Mexico during the 1950s, Hunt managed to plaster the streets of Mexico City with posters encouraging public sentiment against specific government policies, which he achieved by associating them with the communist

---

[11] Edwards was one of the main collaborators of Operation Mockingbird for Latin America. Upon the return of democracy in Chile, in 1993 he received the National Award for Public Relations.

threat. As Edward Bernays had demonstrated years earlier, everything had to be done in the name of third parties, and these had to be individuals or groups with social prestige. The posters were signed by credible organizations that, without realizing it, lent themselves to the maneuver. As Hunt acknowledges in his 2007 memoirs, "these posters, attributed to a respectable institution, had enormous influence among the population."

For the overthrow of Jacobo Árbenz in Guatemala twenty years earlier, the CIA's resources were numerous, but one of them, the invention of agent David Phillips in Chile, was the cacerolazos, later ironically turned into symbols of Latin American leftist resistance. Originally, the CIA had promoted cacerolazos among "housewives" against "communist influence" that was diminishing resources in the kitchens of the subcontinent. In Asia, the CIA preferred to finance pro-Washington films, but in Latin America, written culture carried more weight. The same with graffiti. At least as a planned campaign, the first time it was organized by the CIA: 32 walls and buses were painted in Guatemala against Árbenz, accusing him of being a communist. As is proper, and as dictated by the manual of real conspiracies, each new innovation must be attributed to the adversary.

In other countries, students were accused of responding to an ideology infiltrated from abroad. To top it off, high school students (according to the CIA in Uruguay, university students were a lost cause; they had too much ideological awareness, making them impossible to manipulate, so it was recommended to invest in high school students) put posters on the doors of those who supported Árbenz with the warning: "A communist lives here."

When a representative of the Communist Party of Mexico visited Beijing, Hunt, who is also a prolific novelist, invented a story in which the Mexican envoy denigrated his own compatriots. Proud of a perfect intelligence job, he recalled that he sent it to Washington, where a technical team translated it into Mandarin and copied the typography used by a newspaper in China. When Hunt received the fake copies, he passed them to Mexican journalists with whom he had cultivated a friendly relationship, and the story was translated into Spanish and published. When the affected traveler protested (Hunt never revealed his name), an independent investigation showed that the typography of the leaked newspaper in Mexico and that used by the original in China were the same.

In Mexico, Hunt recruited politicians, students, and priests for his grand mission to overthrow the

$$P - d.t = 0$$

democratic president of Guatemala, Jacobo Árbenz, whom he never stopped calling a dictator. Unlike the financial and political battles, the cultural battle was always won by the left, both in the United States and in Latin America, which is why the idea was implanted that the intellectual world had been infested by Marxism. Paradoxically, the main disruptors of the free process of debate and thought through money and the manipulation of intelligence services were those from Washington and the CIA. Hunt funded Mexican students favorable to his ideology, whom he managed to send to Guatemala to amplify the narrative and the fear of communism.

The CIA not only invested in articles to create direct opinion in the main media outlets across the continent but even in abstract art. In the United States XE "United States" , the Congress for Cultural Freedom, with a presence in dozens of countries, was conceived and funded by the Agency, concerned that not only scientists and writers leaned toward the left but also visual artists.12 In the case of cultural magazines like

---

[12] This foundation operated in 35 countries under the direction of CIA agent Michael Josselson. Due to his Jewish origin, he was persecuted by the Nazis in Europe and, for some reason, in the United States he dedicated himself to persecuting anyone who

the Partisan Review, founded in New York by the Communist Party of the United States in 1934, from the 1950s onward, it was infiltrated by the CIA, which funded it for the following decades. At the same time, the American and Latin American right wings made efforts to propagate the idea that culture had been infiltrated by Marxism long before this current had any relevance in Latin American and American universities.

During this period, apart from radio programs for rural workers, apart from editorials in high-circulation newspapers for the working class and small urban entrepreneurs, cultural magazines held overwhelming influence (something they would never regain) in shaping the opinions of the cultured, rebellious, or leading classes, a minority group but with a relevance that does not exist in the United States. The CIA knows this and knows where to invest its budget surpluses. Various Latin American publications such as *Amaru* from Lima, *Eco* from Bogotá, or *Combate*, founded by the former president of Costa

---

could be suspected of communist sympathies. In his secret catalog were dozens of media outlets and artists for whom he organized exhibitions and promotions regardless of the artistic value of their works.

Rica José Figueres, were funded by the Agency through third parties, such as front foundations, often without the knowledge of their own directors. The magazine *Mundo Nuevo*, founded in Paris by the renowned Uruguayan critic Emir Rodríguez Monegal, was financed by the CIA.[13] The main authors of the Latin American Boom like Octavio Paz, Carlos Fuentes, García Márquez, and Vargas Llosa, as well as those of the alternative Boom, like the Cubans Cabrera Infante and Severo Sarduy, published and were promoted by this influential international publication. With obvious displeasure, Rodríguez Monegal resigned from his position when an investigation by The New York Times revealed this new manipulation by Washington. In issue 14 of Mundo Nuevo, published in August 1967, Rodríguez Monegal (antagonistic, in the famous weekly Marcha from Montevideo to two other respected critics of the continent, the Cuban Fernández Retamar and the Uruguayan Ángel Rama) published a somewhat lukewarm and exculpatory diatribe against the CIA and Stalinism in a long article titled "The CIA and the Intellectuals."

---

[13] The Kaplan Foundation alone donated $35,000 from its own pocket, but it served as a tunnel to transfer over a million dollars from the inflated coffers of the CIA.

His claim that "we are not part of anyone's propaganda" was surely honest, but it was not the truth. It was likely another victim of another plot. The CIA's strategies of plausible deception have a common pattern. In 1972, Rodríguez Monegal was accused of funding the leftist guerrilla movement Tupamaros, of which his daughter was a member. His daughter was detained by the Uruguayan military dictatorship, and he was denied entry into the country until the end of the dictatorship in 1985.

The leak of this operation will trigger an extensive investigation into other practices of the CIA and Washington in other countries, such as coups d'état and the assassinations of troublesome leaders, which will be made possible by a U.S. Congress with a historic number of progressive representatives and congressmen, something that will be reversed in the 1980s with the media, religious, and political reaction of the new neoconservative movement. The CIA and the NSA will also have to rethink how they do things. If before they were academies of secrecy and deception, from now on they will have to go beyond postgraduate studies. Furious over the Senate investigation committees and the declassification of a few secret documents, Secretary of State Henry Kissinger proposes radicalizing measures to prevent future accusations under new standards of "unconditional secrecy." The strategies are endless. According to the National Security Archive, Kissinger himself had leaked secret documents in an attempt to punish the investigative committees, and, according to one of the journalists who uncovered the scandal that led to Nixon's resignation, Carl Bernstein, the same Church Committee omitted more compromising information.

Senator Frank Church will die in 1984 at the age of 59, after spending his last years battling two different cancers, first testicular cancer and then pancreatic cancer. Cancer has frequently been a natural cause of death among dissidents. Of course, these are exaggerated speculations based on mere coincidences. The most powerful intelligence services in the world would never attack the physical integrity of a dissident. Much less one who has exposed them and enjoys some popularity.

During the 1990s, the CIA will heavily invest in films and television programs. Starting in 1996, a veteran of the coup against Allende in Chile, a collaborator of Operation Condor and an expert in psychological warfare, Chase Brandon, will become the CIA's main visual media operator in Latin America. Brandon will act as a producer and advisor for dozens of films, prestigious channels such as Discovery, Learning Channel, and History Channel, and, above all, fast-consumption entertainment programs with mass reach. Not by chance, in the 21st century, the same Agency will continue to kidnap, torture, manipulate information, or pass off innocent deaths as the result of clinical attacks against terrorists in the Middle East with total and absolute impunity.14 On January 31, 2016, The Washington Post will reveal one of the Agency's strategies called Eyewash, which consists of spreading false information not only to the inexperienced public but also to its own second-tier agents, so that no one ever knows whether something is true or the product of some conspiracy theory. In a cable sent to a foreign country, the CIA denounces any operation against target X, and in another, sent to a small circle of officers, it orders them to disregard

---

14 The history of the Guantánamo prison will be only one of the most well-known cases on a long list. For example, in 2019 USA Today will reveal that, following the bombing of Azizabad in Afghanistan on August 22, 2008, U.S. military officials (including Oliver North, convicted and pardoned for lying to Congress in the Iran-Contra scandal) reported that everything had gone perfectly, that the village had welcomed them with applause, that a Taliban leader had been killed, and that collateral damage had been minimal. It was not reported that dozens of people had died, including 60 children. Just a detail.

$$P - d.t = 0$$

any previous information in order to proceed with plan Z. From then on, damned historians will have it harder when they come across some evidence or document. When they discover something, they will be silenced, dismissed by scathing reviews or the mockery of the mocked public.

POST 9/11

HISTORY RHYMED AGAIN in 2003, only this time instead of the *Sedition Act* it was called the Patriot Act, and it not only established direct censorship but also a much worse one: the indirect and often invisible censorship of self-censorship. With a hegemonic power P stagnant or with slower growth, and with a clearly increasing questioning of unidimensional thinking (a d in growth) despite the optimism of The End of History and the end of the tech bubble, tolerance t decreased abruptly. These declines historically translated into restrictive laws on individual freedoms, even in the name of individual freedoms.

More recently, when criticism of racism, patriotic history, and the excessive rights granted to sexual minorities (d_x)—as had been done by the hippies and the anti-Vietnam War movements—began to spread beyond control, the recourse of legal prohibition was revisited. This is the case with the latest laws in Florida, promoted by Governor Ron DeSantis, which directly ban revisionist books and regulate language in schools and public universities—just to start. The creation of a demon called "woke" to replace the loss of the previous demon called "Muslims".

Meanwhile, the stewards, especially the colonial lackeys, continue repeating clichés created generations ago: "How can you live in the United States *and criticize that country? You should move to Cuba, where freedom of expression isn't respected.*" After their clichés, they feel so happy and so patriotic that it's a shame to disturb them with reality.

On May 5, 2023, journalist Julian Assange, imprisoned for over a decade for the crime of having published a minor portion of the atrocities committed by Washington in Iraq, wrote a letter to the new King of England inviting him to visit the depressing Belmarsh Prison in London, where hundreds of prisoners are suffering, some of whom were recognized dissidents. Assange was generously granted the sacred right of freedom of expression, bestowed by the Free World. His letter was published by various Western media outlets, which proves the virtues of the West and the "childish contradictions of those who criticize the Free World from within the Free World." For twelve years, Assange served as an example of lynching. Even during slavery, a few Black people were publicly lynched. The idea was to set an example of what could happen to a truly free society, not to destroy the oppressive order by eliminating all the slaves.

Assange was released in June 2024, after 12 years of confinement and after accepting his guilt as part of a negotiation not without political implications:

The Assange case and the Gaza-Palestine case are two sides of the same coin. Assange's release not only echoes the release of Debs a century ago but also stems from a factual increase (not thanks to power but in spite of power). If d increases and P remains or decreases (as is currently the case), t should decrease as a consequence. However, it is the same power that negotiates an increase in t to balance the equation with an increase in P (in this case, a narrative, moral one).

THE MONITORED FREEDOM OF LIBERTARIANS

IN 2022, THE LIBERTARIAN GOVERNOR of Florida banned 54 math books, claiming they included Critical Race Theory and new pedagogical methods that, according to him, "are not effective," such as Social and Emotional Learning (SEL). He did not explain or discuss which parts of the math books could be antiracist, but he held a press conference in the style of denialist politicians: with furious obviousness about how the universe was created, morality, and the sex of snails.

The media and platforms create a psychological need, and the politicians of denial sell consumers the drug that relieves them—a drug with all the reactionary ingredients imaginable: security, immediacy, victimhood. Some hallucinations are as old as the Theory of White Genocide, invented in the 19th century when Black people became citizens, almost human beings.

This politics of denial deepens and limits the discussion of identity politics (such as the denial of racism; the denial of the existence of gays and lesbians) by hiding the root, such as the existence of class struggle and any form of imperialism itself. If it's not talked about, it doesn't exist.

This product sells so well that, as has been the case for centuries, it has been manufactured and exported to the colonies of the South. For example, the very name "libertarianism," now the banner of rising far-right figures in Latin America like Argentina's Javier Milei, is a literal copy of the "libertarians" who emerged in the United States as a reaction to the humiliating election of a mulatto as president of the United States in 2008. Like the Tea Party, these groups always justify themselves in a tradition they draw from the so-called Founding Fathers. Even in Argentina and Brazil, the yellow flag with the snake that represented the union of the Thirteen Colonies and coiled around the motto "Don't Tread on Me" has been used, though it more resembles a human excrement emoji. Also in Europe, Latin America, and even Hong Kong, right-wing groups have waved the racist and slavery-supporting flag of the Confederacy.

Many Americans who fly this flag on their 4x4s are surprised when reminded that it is the flag of the only group that came close to destroying the country they claim to defend (the United States) with the goal of maintaining slavery and white privilege. Many don't even know this because in this country, raw history is one of the most entrenched taboos.

Not without paradox, it was a conservative libertarian, Texas representative and presidential candidate Ron Paul, who recognized and condemned Washington's imperialist tradition and blamed it for Latin American leaders like Fidel Castro and Hugo Chávez. "We remember nothing, and they forget nothing," he said in a debate. For this insistence, he was silenced by the mainstream media, and many of his followers (including some of my former students, who continue to be politically active) became voters for the socialist Bernie Sanders.

The new label "libertarian" was a strategy known in business: when a company is broken by debt, it is declared bankrupt, renamed, and continues with the same business. The same has happened with neoliberalism. Imposed by the force of arms in Chile with Pinochet and by the force of international banks in dozens of other countries in the '80s and '90s and, more recently, with Mauricio Macri in Argentina and Luis Lacalle Pou in Uruguay, it has always ended in painful failure—not just economic but social. Failure, naturally, not for their class interests.

Libertarian and *neoliberal* are the same thing, but libertarians added the fury of Girolamo Savonarola and Martin Luther. It's the same difference between the calm sermon of a Catholic priest and the sweaty rant of a Protestant pastor. Remember those friendly boys with English accents who preached neighborhood by neighborhood, saving souls (especially their own) back in the '70s and '80s? Well, the seed has borne fruit.

Contrary to the American Founding Fathers, who insisted on separating religion from the state (a legacy of Enlightenment philosophers), libertarians have brought the *missionary* into government. In Brazil, they organized prayers in congress; the president's wife, Bolsonaro's spouse, is an influential pastor; in Costa Rica, a candidate's wife "spoke in tongues" to support the electoral campaign; more recently, deputy Milei argued in the chamber against taxes by citing the Bible: the Jews left Egypt to escape slavery and taxes, just as businessmen now leave Argentina. The list is long and significant.

The politics of denial is the politics of frustrated success: "the right knows how to govern, but has bad luck," which is why it always fails. The feeling of frustration was a reason why so many millions of civilized Europeans supported fascism and Nazism a hundred years ago. If we no longer see it coming, it is because we are inside that suicidal absurdity.

As if all this fanaticism weren't enough, Governor DeSantis, like his Southern imitators now, also insists that professors and civil rights activists indoctrinate the youth, but what indoctrination is more radical than teaching to deny history in the name of God, freedom, the homeland, and family?

What could be more indoctrinating than repeating to children that we are the champions of freedom? That we never invade to defend economic interests but, as Roosevelt and the slaveholders said, out of altruism, to bring freedom to countries of Black people who don't know how to govern themselves. What could be more indoctrinating than denying the horrors of a history for which we are not responsible, but which we adopt when we say "we," and immediately deny that we've done anything wrong?

What could be more radical than presenting the traditional oppressors of class, gender, and other ethnicities as victims?

What could be more radical than Kipling's poem, "The White Man's Burden," the banner of the happy imperialist who carried the Bible in one hand and the whip in the other?

What could be more radical, and what worse indoctrination, than the politics of denial that allows old collective crimes to be committed as if they were new tribal rights?

What could be more radical, dogmatic, doctrinal, and hypocritical than filling podiums with speeches against "cancel culture," furious speeches about freedom, and then, as soon as they come to power, dedicating themselves to passing law after law, prohibiting saying this, discussing that, doing the other? The same hypocrisy of the slaveholders of the United States who defended the expansion of slavery in the name of freedom, order, and civilization. No different from the Latin American dictators promoted by Transnationals, heirs of the powerful Southern slaveholders.

This stale and rejuvenated right, renewed through cosmetic surgery, is so *libertarian* that it only prohibits something when the lower classes threaten to obtain or maintain any right. Always in the name of Law and Order. As Anatole France said, "The law, in its majestic equality, forbids the rich as well as the poor to sleep under bridges, to beg in the streets, and to steal bread."

PSYCHO-PATRIOTISM

BY A 1994 LAW (Holocaust Education Bill), in Florida's public schools, there is a subject called "Holocaust," which studies the racist atrocities that occurred in Europe against the Jewish people. In 2020, Governor Ron DeSantis enacted another law requiring all primary and secondary schools to certify that they are teaching the new generations about the Holocaust. At the time, senators from the African American community ensured that the Ocoee Massacre, where 30 Black people were murdered in 1920, was also included in the curriculum, which, to understand endemic racism and social injustices, is akin to explaining the human body through its shadow.

By law, also, since 2022, in those same Florida secondary schools, it is prohibited to discuss the racist history of the United States. The reason lies, according to Governor Ron DeSantis, in that "no one should be instructed to feel as if they are not equal or ashamed of their race. In Florida, we will not allow the agenda of the extreme left to take over our schools and workplaces. There is no room for indoctrination or discrimination in Florida."

If it is not spoken about, it does not exist. On this side of the Atlantic, racism does not exist and never existed.

The same slavers who defined millions of slaves (the foundation of the country's prosperity) as "private property" based on their skin color called that system a "blessing of slavery," which they wanted to "expand throughout the world" to "fight for freedom," while they called their system of government "democracy" (Brown, 1858).

The same ones who stole from and exterminated native peoples who were far more democratic and civilized than the new nation of the gold rush before the gold rush called it "self-defense" against "unprovoked attacks" by savages (Jackson, 1833; Wayne, 1972).

The same ones who invented the independence of Texas to reinstate slavery and then the war against Mexico to seize half of its territory, the same ones who killed and raped women in front of their children and husbands, did so by the divine will of God's "manifest destiny" (Scott, 1846).

The same people who practiced the sport of killing Black people in the Philippines did it to fulfill "the white man's burden" of civilizing the world (Kipling, 1899).

The same people who invaded, corrupted, and plagued Latin America with banana republics, destroyed democracies, and implanted dozens and dozens of bloody dictatorships, did it to fight for freedom and democracy (Beveridge, 1900; Washington Post, 1920; CIA, XXX).

The same people who showered Asia with atomic bombs, millions of more beneficial bombs without a year of truce, chemical agents on millions of human beings, and left thousands of dead in their wake, called this extreme exercise of racism "heroic victory," even when they were humiliating defeats (Johnson, 1964; Bush, 2003).

But we cannot talk about that because it might offend someone with white skin who feels identified with all those champions of freedom, democracy, and divine justice.

As a popular song used to recruit volunteers for the invented war against Mexico said:

Justice is the motto of our country
the one that is always right (Pratt, 1847).

Not by chance, every time those groups of fanatics felt that their privileges were threatened by the never-accepted equality, they invented theories of self-victimization, such as the theory of "white extermination," articulated in the 19th century to justify colonialism and the oppression of non-Caucasian peoples (Pearson, 1893), and now it has been reborn as a novelty like the "Replacement Theory," which criminalizes immigrants from non-European countries as "dangerous invaders" (Camus, 2010).

Not by chance, Adolf Hitler drew inspiration from the then-institutionalized racism of the American far-right, which indoctrinated millions of people to feel superior because of their skin color and millions more to accept their inferiority for the same reason (Grant, 1916).

Not by chance, Hitler decorated the great businessmen of the United States and forbade the teaching of "leftist things" in public education. Before persecuting and killing Jews, in 1933, he closed the renowned Bauhaus school for being full of "anti-Germans" and being a "refuge for leftists" who wanted to question and change history.

In Florida and across the country, education systems should start with a subject called "Patriotic Hypocrisy" to develop some intellectual capacity to face historical reality without sugarcoating and without the fantasies of Hollywood, Disney World, and the Ku Klux Klan.

We are not responsible for the crimes of our ancestors, but we are responsible for adopting them as our own by denying or justifying them. We are responsible for the crimes and injustices committed today thanks to the denial of reality, which we call patriotism, not without fanaticism. A criminal and racist denial, since, once again, it denies justice and the basic right to the truth of the victims to avoid discomforting the sensitivity of others, the dominant group for more than two centuries, which insists on the strategy of self-complacency and self-victimization as a way to calm their frustrations and foundational hatred. Even worse when that right to the truth has been cut off by laws and a culture full of taboos, all in the name of a democracy that bothers them and which they use, as the demagogues of ancient Athens used it to demonize and then execute Socrates for questioning too much. All done legally, it goes without saying, until the laws are written by others.

What greater indoctrination than denialism or the prohibition of revisiting history? What more indoctrination than imposing complicit silence or a

"patriotic history" in schools, loaded with myths created*post factum* and without documentary support?

THE PROBLEM IS OTHERS' FREEDOM

LET'S START BY REPEATING SOMETHING that has been around for decades: the definition of *pro-life* is not only deeply hypocritical, but it assumes that pro-choice movements are *anti-life*. Even those who define themselves as "pro-choice" do not consider abortion to be good or fun, but rather, in special circumstances, a lesser evil, the result of structural, social, cultural, and individual problems.

In this sense, we can say that the recent decision of the U.S. Supreme Court against the right to abortion in special circumstances (left to the discretion of the states) is just another stop on the path back to the Middle Ages. It is not just a cultural shift (very likely, a reaction to a larger-scale progressive movement toward the expansion of "equal freedom") but, as always, part of a strategy that protects the economic micro-minorities, which at some point will become the center of conflicts and claims of new generations. They know this and need to distract the problem by creating political packages where their political-economic programs go hand in hand with a popular god or some private moral fanaticism, rooted in society. In the Anglo-Saxon world, Protestant, that element must have something sexual and puritanical about it. The warlike crusades that leave millions dead in the name of Christian love are fine.

Last year, Florida Governor Ron DeSantis, the leading contender for the White House in 2024, made headlines with the decision to ban history and math books that referenced Critical Race Theory and any other questioning or revelation about the endemic racism of his country in primary and secondary schools. Similarly, he got the so-called "Don't Say Gay" law approved, according to which the youth of this country can talk about wars, drugs, and rape, but not about the mere existence of people who are a little different from us. Since they, the strange ones, don't meddle in our private lives, we meddle in and legislate over theirs, turning them into taboos that not only destroy the psychology of gay, lesbian, and transgender youth but also put our heterosexual children back into the damned repressive and feared cage of toxic masculinity that we suffered from.

In the same direction and sense is the Supreme Court. Although it is never openly acknowledged, the Supreme Court is a highly political body, which is

why every time one of its nine members dies or re-
tires, a desperate battle begins in Congress to appoint
the new judge according to his ideological orienta-
tion and based on disputes over his sexuality or other
distractions. Most of its members (6 out of 9) were
nominated by conservative presidents of the Republican Party. Five of them were chosen by Presidents
George W. Bush (2) and Donald Trump (3), both of
whom reached the White House after losing the popular vote in the general elections and thanks to an
electoral system designed to protect the slave system
of the sparsely populated (by whites) but powerful
South in the 19th century.

Powerful because of its fanaticism. The same one
that in June 2020 confronted a peaceful protest of
Black citizens protesting against police racism with a
militarized police force and six months later, on January 6, 2021, confronted the white neo-confederates,
armed to the teeth with firearms—another tradition
of the fearful and feared slaveholder South—with the
goal, known by the FBI, of staging a coup d'état by
storming Congress and preventing the confirmation
of the new Democratic president.

This power based on "special rights" of a group
largely composed of the admirers and self-victimized
Confederates and white supremacists, the only group

140

that truly endangered the existence of the very country they now claim to defend like no other. The same ones who fill their mouths with patriotism and strategically accuse critics, the essence of any democracy, of being "anti-American."

That special power of a minority that dogmatically assumes it is the majority encountered a vacancy in the Supreme Court in February 2016, when liberal justice (left, in American parlance) Antonin Scalia passed away. It fell to Democratic President Barack Obama to nominate a replacement, who would, obviously, align with his political views. The Republicans blocked this nomination for almost a year until the new Republican president, Donald Trump, was in the White House and could nominate the conservative Neil Gorsuch.

The last member to join the Supreme Court confirms this reasoning. On September 18, 2020, just over a month before the general elections that Joe Biden would win, liberal Justice Ruth Ginsburg died. The Republicans managed to nominate and approve their conservative candidate, Amy Coney Barrett, in record time on October 27, 2020, days before the elections.

Due to this decision by the Court (a highly political body predominantly composed of men), the

CDC, a government agency, estimates that Black women will experience a 33 percent increase in deaths related to pregnancy. For thousands of women, pregnancy will mean a death sentence.

What's next on this path to the Middle Ages? One of the Supreme Court justices, the ultra-conservative Clarence Thomas, made it clear in writing: *"In future cases, we should reconsider all substantive due process precedents of this Court, including Griswold* [1965, concerning the use of contraceptives], *Lawrence* [2003, against the criminalization of homosexuality] *and Obergefell* [2015, in favor of same-sex marriage]."

In other words, the veteran conservative of the Supreme Court stated that the next steps toward this neomedievalism will be to prohibit same-sex marriages, criminalize different sexual orientations, and ban the use of contraceptive pills.

If we continue down this path of historical regression, the next step would be the prohibition of divorce and interracial marriage, which was illegal until the Supreme Court lifted its ban in 1967, when Justice Thomas was 19 years old.

Of course, this goal of the converted Savonarola could face an obstacle. The justice, a hero for Protestant conservatives, Catholics, and white supremacists, is a Black man (or "African American," though in practice he is less African American than the white Elon Musk) and is married, for the second time, to the conservative activist Ginni Lamp, a blonde woman, a member of the Tea Party, and founder of Liberty Central and Liberty Consulting.

The word *liberty* is so beautiful. Who could be against freedom? Everyone loves freedom.

As long as it's not someone else's freedom, of course.

BANNING IDEAS IN THE NAME OF FREE SPEECH

IN LINE WITH THE PRESIDENT of Brazil, Captain Jair Bolsonaro, the governor of Florida, Ron DeSantis, signed a law allowing university students to record professors to detect any ideological tendencies. As long as it wasn't the true ideology. In December of that year, the governor signed another bill to *"give businesses, employees, children, and families the tools they need to fight against the so-called WOKE indoctrination"* (*"woke,"* in African American dialect), which proposes a re-reading of history from the perspective of groups marginalized by power. For the *fanatics*, taking a five-year-old child to a religious temple every week or planting them in front of the television for four hours a day to consume mercantilist propaganda is not indoctrination. But if a 20-year-old enters a university where they might learn some new idea, then that is "indoctrination" and "brainwashing."

The law that bans an open discussion about racism (the time will come to prohibit the word *imperialism*) because white young people might feel uncomfortable studying slavery and discrimination was added to another law from the same office, which prohibits public high schools from speaking about the existence of gay and lesbian people in the name of a fight "against gender ideology." The dominant gender ideology for centuries, machismo, is not up for debate. On the contrary, it must be protected through fanatical ignorance.

A specialty of the champions of freedom is to prohibit everything that doesn't align with their interests, such as the *Individual Freedom Law* which prohibits any company from requiring its employees to take anti-racism awareness courses. Their repeated "freedom of expression" is freedom to harass and censor. This tsunami of prohibitions in education and academia is only the continuation of the ban on dozens of books that began earlier in the United States, in the best banana republic style. This same ideology, with its phrases and tics copied from American libertarians, is repeated as a copy-and-paste across Latin America, echoing the articles and doctrines planted by the CIA in dozens of countries, which germinated, matured, and continue to bear fruit decades after the Cold War.

Sooner or later, they were going to come for the universities. It is the greatest thorn in the side of the

Successful Businessmen and their butlers. Culture and universities have not been easy to buy, although corporations have done a good job of commercializing education and research. According to conservative fanatics, universities are bastions of liberals (leftists) where young people are indoctrinated. They complain that most professors are left-wing and that, therefore, legislation is needed to balance the proportion of conservatives. There is no similar proposal to balance ideologies in the powerful churches, in the multimillion-dollar corporations, in the stock markets, in the powerful lobbies of Washington, or in the unlimited donations to political parties.

The natural solution to balance political tendencies in universities is for the Future Businessmen to finally sit down and study seriously for once in their damn lives. But of course, if someone loves money and power, they're unlikely to invest decades doing research for free. Especially knowing that, after decades of others' efforts, when the results appear, the Successful Businessmen will immediately hijack them in the name of Freedom.

In theory, fascism and liberalism are opposites. However, decades ago, neoliberalism (economic) managed to combine a diverse menu into one package. Thus, in the same party, you had the most radical capitalists and warmongers alongside Christians who had nothing to do with the Jesus of the Gospels, but rather with Judas, someone who could sell out his own friend for thirty pieces of silver. Thus, defending Jesus meant defending the merchants unjustly expelled from the temple, forcing the damned camel through the eye of the damned needle, and supporting the empires that crucified other rebels. The lords of money, the boards of corporations that spread banana dictatorships around the world and legalized dictatorships in their own countries, all in the name of freedom and democracy as in the times of slavery, managed to unite the two opposing ideologies. The neoliberals of the latter half of the 20th century are the libertarians of today and drink at the bar with neo-Nazis and neo-fascists with total comfort.

Of course, not everyone is a fan of the Holy Office. In August 2022, federal judge Mark Walker blocked (temporarily) Florida's "Anti-WOKE" law, arguing that, according to the law, *"professors can exercise their 'academic freedom' as long as they express only those views approved by the State."* Logical, but provisional. A month later, Governor De Santis swept the elections. He was reelected governor and positioned himself as one of the strongest Republican candidates for the 2024 presidential election.

Every time a conservative politician stirs the wrath of the Inquisition, they achieve excellent results. Which proves, once again, that we continue marching toward a new Middle Ages. All with the silence, timidity, or complicity of academia and what was once the heroic resistance for Civil Rights.

While some academics are too preoccupied with a model that explains inflation in the Maldives or how to cite Socrates in a journal no one will read, the Businessmen continue with their plans to neutralize or take control of one of the last corners of society they have not yet fully dominated, despite the commercialization of education. I've heard that, "Well, that's the job of the professors." That is, they shouldn't concern themselves with big politics. It's not their thing.

The same isn't said about a successful casino owner or a pillow salesman aspiring to be governor or president. No, because Successful Businessmen are used to commanding and being successful... Not a few professors remain silent, fearing what is repeated in assemblies and hallways as *"fear of retaliation"* for speaking their minds. Even the *"tenured"* fear protesting, despite being legally untouchable.

In the United States, tenure was created in 1940 to prevent professors from being fired for their radical or inconvenient ideas and opinions. For the same reason, tenure has been under attack in this country for years. Not only is there an attempt to eliminate it, but it has been reduced to a minimum, with a dual purpose: (1) to precarious academic work (depressing salaries) and (2) to silence theories inconvenient to the dominant dogma.

But tenured professors fear other forms of retaliation. For example, the reduction of their salaries, something that authorities later fail to explain without resorting to childish excuses based on the dominant dogma, such as the Law of Supply and Demand… As if that law weren't loaded with politics.

In this way, we teachers are also neutralized in our ethical commitment to the rest of society, to transformative knowledge, to challenging established norms, and to fighting for a better society and world.

DIXIE'S LAND

AS HISTORY SUGGESTS, the reaction of a power (P) under scrutiny due to the uncontrolled growth of dissent-diversity (d) led to a backlash against tolerance for that dissent-diversity and a sharp decrease in tolerance (t) through laws, just as it happened during the 19th century when the wave of abolitionist activism and opinion began to threaten the existence of the powerful slave system in the South.

In 2022, Florida Governor Ron DeSantis banned 54 math textbooks, claiming they included Critical Race Theory and new pedagogical methods that, according to him, "are not effective," such as Social and Emotional Learning (SEL). He neither explained nor discussed which paragraphs of the math textbooks could be anti-racist, but he held a press conference in the style typical of denialist politicians: with furious obviousness about how the universe was created, morality, and the sex of snails.

Governor DeSantis made headlines with his decision to ban history and math textbooks that referenced the*Critical Theory of Race* and any other questioning or revelation about the endemic racism of his country in primary and secondary schools. That same year, the governor successfully pushed for the approval of the "Parental Rights in Education Act," known as "Don't Say Gay," according to which young people in this country can talk about wars, drugs, and rapes, but not about the mere existence of people who are a bit different from us. Since these invisible "others" don't interfere in our private lives, we interfere and legislate on theirs, turning them into taboos that not only damage the psychology of young gay, lesbian, and transgender individuals but also trap our heterosexual children once again in the dreaded, repressive cage of toxic masculinity that we ourselves have suffered.

A year earlier, in 2021, Florida Governor Ron DeSantis, in line with the neofascist president of Brazil, Captain Jair Bolsonaro, had passed a law allowing university students to record professors to detect any ideological bias. As long as it wasn't the true ideology. In December of that year, the governor signed another bill to *"give businesses, employees, children, and families the tools necessary to fight against the indoctrination called WOKE"* (*"awake"*, in African-American dialect), which proposes a re-reading of history from the perspective of groups marginalized from power. For the fanatics, taking a five-year-old to a religious temple every week or planting them in front of the television for four hours a day to consume mercantilist propaganda is not indoctrination. But if a 20-year-old enters a university where they might learn some new ideas, then that is indeed "indoctrination" and "brainwashing."

The law that prohibits an open discussion about racism (the time will come to ban the word *imperialism*) because young white people might feel uncomfortable studying slavery and discrimination, was added to another law from the same office, which prohibits public high schools from speaking about the existence of gays and lesbians in the name of a fight "against gender ideology." The dominant gender ideology for centuries, machismo, is not up for discussion. On the contrary, it must be protected through fanatical ignorance.

Sooner or later, they were going to come for the universities. They are the biggest thorn in the side of the Successful Businessmen and their stewards. Culture and universities have not been easy to buy, although corporations have done a good job commercializing education and research. According to conservative fanatics, universities are liberal (leftist) strongholds where the youth are indoctrinated.

They complain that most professors are leftist and that, therefore, legislation must be enacted to balance the proportion of conservatives. No such proposal exists to balance ideologies in powerful churches, billionaire corporations, stock exchanges, powerful lobbies in Washington, or in the unlimited donations to political parties.

Of course, not everyone is a fanatic of the Holy Office. In August 2022, federal judge Mark Walker temporarily blocked Florida's "Anti WOKE" law, arguing that, according to the law, *"professors can exercise their 'academic freedom' as long as they only express viewpoints approved by the State."* Logical, but provisional. A month later, Governor DeSantis swept the elections. He was reelected governor and positioned himself as one of the strongest Republican candidates for the 2024 presidential race.

In another state with a deep Hispanic history celebrated and tragedies of dispossession obsessively repressed, Texas, in 2021 also passed a law limiting and controlling discussions on racial issues and slave history in schools. Out of fear, some professors suspended certain classes and modified their syllabi to avoid lawsuits, dismissals, or criticism from parents.

Although the language of the law was cloaked in politically correct rhetoric, such as the prohibition of not mentioning that "one race or sex is inherently superior to another race or sex," the objective was to interrupt a growing discussion about the country's racist history and the sexism of the dominant discourse. Nothing better than banning the word "black" to halt the revision of a discourse where "black" appears, deceitfully and unacademically, a million times in the press and in transcripts of Congress and the White House.

In May 2023, Texas lawmakers voted to require that the biblical Ten Commandments be posted in all public school classrooms to rescue the morality of the Empire. It's not uncommon to see these *tablets* in the town halls of some towns in other Dixie states. McCarthyism is back. The so-called Founding Fathers turned in their graves. The crusaders and the Inquisition celebrated forced conversion, even though they have yet to apply the Judas Cradle to their own citizens, as it is applied in torture centers without laws, like Guantanamo or the many secret prisons the CIA maintains in the seas and various countries.

These are just new signs of the decline of an empire that doesn't know where it's going and can't see the world and its solutions in any other way than it has done since the 17th century. Meanwhile, in its neocolonies, the lackeys keep shouting "freedom, freedom!" like a rosary prayer.

A year later, in June 2024, another state of the Dixie, Louisiana, passed a law requiring public schools to display the Ten Commandments (biblical) in large letters on their walls. In contradiction to the Constitution and against all the writings of the revered Founding Fathers like Thomas Jefferson, the governor of the southern state justified the decision: *"If you want to respect the rule of law, you must start from the original law given, which was Moses. ... He received his commandments from God,"* said Governor Landry.

We return to $t = P/d$. Clearly and in all cases, it is a reaction against the "dangerous growth" of d, which produces a dramatic reduction of t to preserve a weakened and nervous P.

THE PRICE OF NOT BEING A COLONY

NOW LET'S LOOK AT THOSE COUNTEREXAMPLES of hegemonic power and its stewards. Why don't you go to Cuba where people don't have freedom of expression, where there is no pluralism of political parties?

To begin with, it would be necessary to point out that all political systems are exclusionary, though to varying degrees. In Cuba they do not allow liberal parties to participate in their elections, which are labeled as a farce by liberal democracies. In countries with liberal democratic systems, such as the United States, elections are essentially elections of a single party called the Democratic-Republican Party. There is no possibility of a third party seriously challenging the One Party because it is the party of corporations, which are the elite that holds the real power in the country. On the other hand, if, for example, in a country like Uruguay a Marxist like José Mujica wins the elections, or in Chile another Marxist like Gabriel Boric wins, no sensible person would even imagine that those presidents were going to step outside the constitutional framework to turn those countries into Soviet-style systems prohibited by the constitutions of those countries. The same happens in Cuba, but it must always be said that it is not the same.

Now, let's return to the logic of freedom of expression in different systems of global power. To summarize, I believe it is necessary to consider that freedom of expression is a luxury that, historically, colonies or republics struggling for independence from the empires have not been able to afford. It would suffice to remember the example of Guatemalan democracy, destroyed by the Great Democracy of the United States in 1954 because its government, democratically elected, decided to enforce the sovereign laws of its own country, which did not suit the megacorporation United Fruit Company. The Great Democracy did not hesitate to install another dictatorship, which left hundreds of thousands dead over decades. The same story in Iran, Chile, Congo, Indonesia, Burkina Faso... Only limiting ourselves to the Cold War.

What was the main *problem* of Guatemalan democracy in the 50s? It was its freedom of the press, its freedom of expression. Because of this, the Northern Empire and the UFCo managed to manipulate public opinion in that country through a deliberately planned propaganda campaign acknowledged by its own perpetrators—not by their Creole stewards, it goes without saying.

When this occurred, the young Argentine doctor, Ernesto Guevara, was in Guatemala and had to flee into exile in Mexico, where he met other exiles, the Cubans Fidel and Raúl Castro. When the Cuban Revolution triumphed, Ernesto Guevara, by then El Che, summed it up remarkably: "Cuba will not be another Guatemala." What did he mean by this? Cuba would not allow itself to be inoculated like Guatemala through "free press." History proved him right: When in 1961 Washington invaded Cuba based on the CIA's plan that assured "Cuba will be another Guatemala," it failed spectacularly. Why? Because its population did not join the "liberating invasion," as it could not be inoculated by the massive propaganda allowed by the "free press." Kennedy knew it and reproached the CIA, which threatened to dissolve and ended up dissolved.

THE END OF HISTORY

FOLLOWING THE SUICIDE OF THE SOVIET UNION came an orgy of liberal optimism. But this was rather rhetorical. While liberal elites pocketed as much as they could from a wave of aggressive privatizations across the world, a ghost haunted the party hall. What if people ended up believing that democracy is the power of the people and began demanding social rights and a greater democratization of the economy that was never democratic?

It was at this point that, in reaction to a visibly d_a weakened, a potential d_b began to grow and, above all, to project itself as a force out of control, despite the mask of the "single model." All this despite the abrupt growth of hegemonic power P. Not by chance, the paradigmatic and apologetic book The End of History and the Last Man (1992) by Professor Francis Fukuyama was followed by another equally paradigmatic and apocalyptic book by another professor, Samuel Huntington: The *Clash of Civilizations and the Remaking of World Order* (1996). The book *The Wild Frontier: 200 Years of Anglo-Saxon Fanaticism in Latin*

America that we published in 2021 summarizes this moment with a chapter whose title captures this idea: "1998. The Winners Feel Insecure." This chapter referenced the Project for the New American Century (PNAC), which had decided that the removal of Saddam Hussein should be "the goal of US foreign policy." Three weeks later, on February 19, in an interview for NBC's Today Show, Bill Clinton's Secretary of State, Madeleine Albright, clarified: if for that "we must use force, we will use it, because we are the United States; we are the indispensable nation; we can look higher and further into the future than any other nation." In February 2003, against the UN and massive protests worldwide, the United States, England, and Spain (according to its president José María Aznar, desperate to "get out of the corner of history") would make the longed-for invasion of Iraq a reality under the pretext that the Iraqi dictator possessed weapons of mass destruction. When these weapons failed to appear anywhere, despite years of searching and a million deaths in the adventure, the leaders of the three countries would admit that they had faulty information and that, in any case, the massacre and destabilization of the Middle East wasn't such a bad idea since it promoted democracy in the region. They won't say they lied because it looks bad, and honesty won't get them that far. It will all be reduced to an apology, which is what the powerful do, at best.

Among the members of the PNAC were the neoconservative writer Robert Kagan, the professors Francis Fukuyama and Donald Kagan, the future Vice President Dick Cheney, the future Secretary of State Donald Rumsfeld, the future Secretary of Defense Paul Wolfowitz and the future National Security Advisor to Donald Trump, John Bolton. The report published by the PNAC, "Rebuilding America's Defenses (Reconstructing the defenses of the United States)", demonstrates that, even though the U.S. military is by far the most expensive and powerful in the world, Washington did not feel secure. Militarism, revived as a reaction to the sixties in the United States, had consolidated itself as a material and ideological reality, but the neoconservatives were not satisfied. The PNAC lobby, among its recommendations, established that the U.S. military should eliminate any competition anywhere in the world. The regime of Saddam Hussein in Iraq had to be removed by force, and the entire Middle East had to be redesigned according to Washington's plan. However, convincing the American people to support the actions that would make this plan possible would take a long time, unless there were to be a *"process of transfor-*

mation, even if it brings revolutionary change, is likely to be a long one, absent some catastrophic and catalyzing event—like a new Pearl Harbor."[15]

After the Church Commission and the most critical Congress in the history of the United States approved some laws limiting the powers of the CIA to assassinate at will, in 2001 President George W. Bush approved a resolution by which the CIA and other agencies would grant themselves the right to be both judge and executioner, eliminating individuals and deciding on massacres in the name of the fight against terrorism. As investigative journalist Evan Wright would explain (echoing CIA manuals from the Cold War era), the mechanism that unleashed government commandos and private companies like Blackwater to assassinate without a presidential order aimed to keep public figures (the politicians who receive votes) immaculate from any criminal responsibility.[16]

---

[15] On page 51, the document states, *"Further, the process of transformation, even if it brings revolutionary change, is likely to be a long one, absent some catastrophic and catalyzing event—like a new Pearl Harbor"*.

[16] Among the mercenaries of these government groups will be the Cuban Enrique (Ricky) Prado, another resident of the beaches of Miami and accused of unresolved murders, who will climb the ranks in the CIA until reaching SIS-2. Blackwater,

---

recipient of hundreds of millions of dollars from Washington, is a private army founded by the ultra-conservative Christian Erik Prince, brother of the future Secretary of Education under President Donald Trump, Betsy DeVos.

POWER FORGETS ITS LAWS

ON JULY 13, 1854, THE NAVY of the United States bombed San Juan in Nicaragua until it was wiped off the map to, according to Captain Hollins, give the Nicaraguans "a lesson that will never be forgotten." This brutality was a response to a minor incident in the country's waters. A modern all-iron steamship, the H. L. Routh, had collided with a small merchant boat on the San Juan River. The wooden bungo, owned by Don Antonio Paladino, had suffered significant damage, so Paladino had insulted the captain of the steamship. The captain of the Routh, T.T. Smith, did not understand the insults in the local language, but he understood the tone, and he threatened to whip him, a common practice among civilized slaveholders. According to the testimony of some passengers from California, the Routh seemed to have lost its rudder and had veered from its course eleven miles from San Juan. Minutes after the collision and the insults, the Routh reversed and returned to the small wooden boat. Offended and furious, armed with a rifle, Captain Smith shot the insolent Paladino. One of the bullets pierced his chest. Not satisfied, Smith rammed the wooden bungo until it was in pieces. On board, the members of the Accessory Transit Company of New York, the owners of the Routh, returned to their tables. Apart from some protests from a few passengers, nothing had happened.

The next day, with a judicial order in hand, the commissioner of San Juan del Norte attempted to arrest Captain Smith on charges of murder. One of the passengers of the Routh, the plenipotentiary minister of the United States in Central America, former senator of Arkansas and future fighter for the racist southern Confederacy, Solon Borland, refused to read the arrest warrant and (according to the Pittsburgh Gazette of May 30) decreed that the officials of Nicaragua "have no authority to arrest a United States citizen, no matter the crime he may have committed. "Borland was better armed than the Nicaraguan officials and ordered the commissioner (a skinny Black man whose name has vanished from the annals of history, though the reference to his race remains) to go back where he came from. The commissioner and his officials retreated.

This story repeated itself in various forms for over a century, not only in Latin America. For example, on July 21, 2020, the Trump administration issued an arrest warrant and a $5 million bounty for the capture of the president of Venezuela's Supreme Court, Maikel Moreno, accused of corruption. Secretary of State Mike Pompeo explained the decision: Moreno "accepted bribes to influence the outcomes of certain criminal cases in Venezuela; with this announcement, we are sending a clear message: the United States stands against corruption." In August 2001, in response to the request by Spanish judge Baltasar Garzón for former Secretary of State Henry Kissinger to testify before international courts regarding his involvement in Latin American dictatorships, the George W. Bush administration released a statement protesting: "It is unfair and ridiculous for a distinguished servant of this country to be harassed by foreign courts. The danger of the International Criminal Court is that one day U.S. citizens might be arrested abroad for political motivations, as in this case."

Despite the fact that a record of brutality, violence, violation of international law, destruction of foreign democracies, and the annihilation of millions of people through all types of bombings—from conventional to illegal, such as chemical agents—has been an established, practiced, and honored tradition by nearly every U.S. president, none have ever been brought to trial. None of them ever faced removal from their position through impeachment. Richard Nixon resigned earlier over a minor scandal compared to his long record of political crimes, leaving his position of power to his vice president. All the others were venerated and honored for their crimes.

The first former president who had to face a jury and a court was Donald Trump. The long list of illegal acts, or at least those that warranted investigation, made the job quite easy for the journalists and prosecutors of the time, to the historic extent that in June 2024 he was found guilty of the crime of falsifying documents related to his private businesses, especially those related to tax evasion or falsifying data in his declarations. The more serious accusations, such as attempting to rig the 2020 elections or inciting a revolt against Congress while it was trying to confirm the winner of those elections, Joe Biden, were halted by a swift resolution from the Supreme Court of the United States. Six of the nine judges voted in favor of recognizing immunity for President Trump in his actions as president, a decision that represents one more step (in fact, several more steps) in the long trend of increasing presidential power in the American system after the Second World War.[VI]

This court ruling increases the power of the presidents of the United States, whether Republican or

Democrat. That is, it increases the executive power of the single party for economic and financial power. One more step toward the increase of Western P to the detriment of t and against d in $P = dt$.

Challenged and cornered by d, the hegemonic power becomes a banana republic power and proceeds to crush the t using methods previously reserved for its colonies.

LYING IS OUR PROFESSION

ON APRIL 15, 2019, RECLINING in a leather chair on the stage of the auditorium at Texas A&M University, Secretary of State Mike Pompeo listens to a question from a student, who asks him to explain the policies of sanctions against some countries and concessions to other regimes like that of Saudi Arabia. The secretary begins to speak about how tough the world out there is as a way to find the answer. He doesn't find it, but a thought occurs to him that he finds amusing. With an uncontrollable inner laugh that shakes his three hundred pounds of body weight, he asks: "What is the motto of the cadets at the West Point military academy? 'You will not lie, cheat, or steal, nor tolerate those who do'. Well, I was the director of the CIA and I can assure you that we lie, cheat, and steal. We have entire courses of training for that. It reminds us of the greatness of the American experiment." The rest of the audience rewards him with laughter and applause.

Fake news was popular even before Texas's independence *in 1836 and multiplied during the war against Mexico* starting in 1844. By the end of the 19th century, with the invention of yellow journalism in New York, it became a massive and more refined strategy to increase sales by inventing the war against Spain *in 1898. At the beginning of the 20th century, fake news was systematized by Edward Bernays*, which helped sell U.S. intervention in World War I and coups d'état like in Guatemala in 1954. The CIA used public opinion manipulation as its primary weapon and did so in various ways, planting editorials in major regional newspapers shortly before a military intervention or to secure the condemnation, blockade, or harassment of any president not aligned with Washington's policies and the interests of multinational corporations.

Organizations, foundations, and agencies created with this goal have been numerous and diverse, though with certain common characteristics. In the 1980s, with the approval of President Ronald Reagan, Cuban Otto Reich created the Office of Public Diplomacy for Latin America, which had to be closed in 1989 when its practices of manipulating public opinion through Pentagon funds and the CIA leaked to the public. The Office collaborated with the CIA's psychological operations department and reported directly to the White House through Colonel Oliver North. One of its strategies was to plant op-eds in major media outlets and fake intelligence leaks to influence the public, creating panic or fear towards groups like the Sandinistas in Nicaragua and presenting the Contras as heroic "freedom fighters."[17] Reich had invented that Soviet planes had arrived in Nicaragua, that the regime already possessed chemical weapons, and that it was involved in drug trafficking, with such success that voices in Congress began calling for an air strike on Managua. It would take the more serious journalists a few years to discover that the information they received from "reliable sources" was a crude manipulation.

The *Office* was closed for spreading covert propaganda and false information using State Department funds without congressional approval. Its crime was

---

[17] Among the media outlets that published the fabrications of The Office were the *Miami* Herald, Newsweek, the Wall Street Journal, the Washington Post, the New York Times, and several television networks like NBC. Information favorable to the government of Nicaragua will be discredited as "Sandinista propaganda." Otto Reich and various leaks from his Office explain that this distortion of information was due to U.S. journalists receiving sexual favors from the Nicaraguan government—women when the journalists were heterosexual and gay men when they were gay.

P - d.t = 0

not manipulating public opinion with fake news but using money it shouldn't have. On September 7, 1988, the State Department, in a secret document, records that the plan of *"this group of individuals"* is to influence public opinion through the press and secure a congressional vote in the United States favorable to their interests. This group would maintain bank accounts in the Cayman Islands and Swiss banks (used to launder money from the arms sale to Iran through Israel) with the collaboration of Colonel Oliver North. Otto Juan Reich will continue working as an advisor to Presidents Bush Sr. and Bush Jr., and in 2012, he will receive the Walter Judd Freedom Award.[18]

The weapon of manipulating public opinion will never be abandoned, no matter the revelations against it. Among other powerful organizations, the Rendon Group will continue this tradition. The Pentagon will pay Rendon to propagate false information

---

[18] Although the Cuban exile represents a tiny fraction of the entire Hispanic population in the United States (four percent of the Hispanic population if all Cubans in this country are considered), their representation and political power is almost absolute in the CIA and in various trade bodies, and major in the media, politics, and the U.S. Congress.

as a weapon of war. The strategy resembles that practiced by Edward Bernays during the last century: having someone with a certain prestige and not linked to us (doctors, religious leaders, established media outlets) say what they want people to believe, thus defending freedom and democracy. Rendon manages to leak and plant information that will be published by "independent journalists," some of whom are on the Pentagon's payroll. John Rendon, hired to manipulate public opinion about the war in Iraq, will boast: "I can tell you what will be tomorrow's headline in any country in the world." His payroll includes 195 newspapers in 43 countries that reproduce his ideas.

Any of the founders of the Association for Responsible Dissent (ARDIS; its members included former Marines, ex-CIA agents, and FBI agents, among others), would have added that Secretary Pompeo forgot to mention that we not only "lie, cheat, and steal" but also kill. In 1987, ARDIS estimated that "at least six million people died as a result of the covert operations of the United States since World War II… people who weren't even at war with the United States," all done "in the name of the American people." The group also denounced the recruitment of candidates on university campuses by the CIA, a practice that continues today, more or less secretly.

$$P - d.t = 0$$

BIBLICAL PATRIOTISM. SAVING THE SERMON AT ANY COST

IN FEBRUARY 2023, THE SUPREME COURT of the United States refused to review a law in the state of Arkansas requiring all government contractors to swear loyalty to Israel, like the 2022 law in Georgia that demands loyalty to Israel from any large contractor doing business with the state. By 2024, 37 out of the 50 states in the Union had regulations requiring oaths of loyalty to a foreign state, Israel.

At the end of 2023, amidst the massacre of Palestinian men, women, and children in Gaza by Israel, one of the best disciples of the American South, Germany, began discussing a law requiring candidates for naturalization as citizens of that country to swear loyalty to the same foreign state, Israel.

By June of the same year, Germany determined that applicants for naturalization must affirm Israel's right to exist, without mentioning any right of existence for Palestinians or for Palestine as a country.

The war in Gaza and Berlin's strong support for Israel have fueled many discussions in Germany.

Chancellor Olaf Scholz declared that Israel's security is a "raison d'état" for Germany.[VII]

In few parts of the world since World War II has there been such a dramatic collapse of the global narrative consensus as in Palestine during the 2023-2024 massacre. This is a verifiable fact beyond any opinion. As Israel reduces Gaza to dust and obliterates any right or sense of humanity in Palestine, the dominant narrative of the world's major media crumbles, turning into an inverse Gaza.

As a logical consequence of $P = d.t$ and that overwhelming d that seems unstoppable, Western governments, hegemonic powers, declining empires (for various reasons we cannot analyze now) rush to hammer against t.

CENSORSHIP IN THE FREE WORLD

THE SO-CALLED *FREE WORLD*, one of the most success-ful and massive advertising slogans in history, refers to those countries allied with liberal democracies and dictatorial economies that were part of or participated in centuries of imperialism and slavery. Paradoxically, but not by coincidence, it is generally democracies that have been and continue to be, those which en-force *their laws within and beyond their borders*.

As we saw in the chapter "Freedom of Expression in Times of Slavery," the most effective and extensive censorship is not exercised by prohibiting ideas, but by demonizing them. When this tactic proves ineffec-tive, direct prohibition is resorted to, as in the case of the Inquisition or certain states in the Southern United States, like Florida, where laws ban hundreds of books, courses in public universities, and even ways of speaking or viewing the world in secondary schools—all in the name of freedom.

But generally, in liberal democracies, censorship does not need to be exercised directly and overtly, as in more traditional dictatorships. In fact, a censorship that allows room for dissent is much more effective, as it is harder to perceive and denounce. "How can you say there's censorship if you're saying it?" "How can you say there's a private dictatorship if you can criticize it without going to prison, as in North Korea?" To then conclude with one of the favorite expressions exuded by the system through its vassals and stewards: "If you criticize this system so much, why don't you go live in North Korea?" This is only the surface of a deeply authoritarian mindset.

But true freedom of expression is not measured by the ability to say what an individual wants, including the most cathartic insults a soccer fan might shout from the stands, but by the ability to say something that could induce real change in real power. If we publicly assert that the real power in the world lies with corporations and the owners of finance in Wall Street and London, we will have no problem in the Free World until that assertion translates into a threat to that power. For example, if the emergence of a new collective consciousness is detected. Then, at first, servile media outlets discredit the critic (with their "*equal* right to reply"); then secret agencies, with less legal tools. The last and least convenient step is to imprison the critic, as in the case of Edward Snowden, or make them disappear, as has been the case for many, both in the satellite dictatorships of Latin America and Africa as well as within the Free World itself.

The censorship of the strategically named Free World is not based on *prohibition* but on the *marginalization* of any narrative, information, or criticism that might threaten the consensus radiating from the center. Dissidents are an involuntary and, probably, inevitable part of that mechanism. When the margin threatens to destabilize the center, direct censorship appears, as in the case of the laws passed since 2020 in Florida banning hundreds of books, courses, and words as far as it is possible to prohibit—all in the name of the freedom of the supposed victims, that is, those (subjects of the center) who might feel uncomfortable by the truths and sufferings of others.

The center needs the dissent of the margin (within tolerable and functional limits) for two reasons: one, as a way to legitimize its self-congratulatory narratives about freedom, democracy, and tolerance of others' opinions; two, as a always available resource of antagonistic forces, that is, once the margin threatens to destabilize the discursive hegemony of the center, it is reclaimed as a demon or a danger to the destruction of freedom and civilization. Often, the center uses individuals from the margin elevated to the status of examples of the superiority of the center: Blacks who whip other disobedient Black slaves; Indians who beat their children to make them respect the symbols of the conqueror; satisfied poor who criticize other hungry poor for not working hard enough; immigrants who attack other immigrants over some difference, such as legal status, because they need to be two hundred percent European or American to be considered sixty percent European or American.

The effects of this perfect systematic and depersonalized censorship (like almost everything in capitalism) are also two: the majorities panic and rush toward the center of power dominated by an ideological and financial elite (generally, the ideological right) or the most prominent representatives of the margin propose policies, solutions, and positions called "centrist" (in a political and ideological sense) which, if successful in some electoral process, will be quickly reconquered by the center of power (the right, in the West) through the force of its financial resources, of the propaganda of the dominant media and myths such as "the responsibility and pragmatism" of the new rebel leader, now tamed by the establishment. This, generally, is the only possibility for a leader who comes from the margins to the political (not economic) center in order not to succumb in any

of their attempts at moderate reforms that simultane-
ously manage to calm the frustrations of the population and keep the elite of real power in their castles.
To avoid being removed from political power, or sab-
otaged, the rebel, even if they represent an overwhelming majority of the population, must negotiate
with the one percent who hold economic-media
power and, often, military power.

As George Orwell summarized in an unpublished
preface to *Animal Farm* (1945), *"The sinister fact about
literary censorship in England is that it is largely voluntary. Unpopular ideas can be silenced and inconvenient
facts kept dark, without the need for any official ban. Anyone who has lived long in a foreign country will know of
instances of sensational news items, things which on their
own merits would make big headlines, being kept out of
the British press, not because the government intervened,
but a general consensus, a tacit agreement that something
'would not do' to be mentioned. As far as newspapers go,
this is easy to understand. The British press is extremely
centralized and most of it is owned by wealthy men who
have every reason for being dishonest on important issues.
The same veiled censorship also operates in books and pe-
riodicals, as well as in plays, films, and radio".*"[VIII]

IF NOT BY PROPAGANDA, IT WILL BE BY LAW

ON MAY 1, 2024, the US House of Representatives passed the Antisemitism Awareness Act. The urgency was due to the massive protests against the genocide in Gaza taking place on dozens of university campuses.

From then on, any public or academic discussion about what is or is not antisemitism was definitively defined *by law*, which grants the Secretary of Education, Miguel Cardona, greater power to determine punishments and sanctions, according to their high discretion, on what constitutes antisemitism and what the correct resolution is to the ethical dilemma of the trolley problem. Any discussion must now be framed within the boundaries set by the leader of the Free World and *"shall not be subject to interpretation"* (Sec. 6-a).

The new law was justified based on the *Civil Rights Act* of 1964, which prohibits discrimination against individuals based on race or national origin, which is a magnificent expression of hypocrisy, considering that this law was the product of mobilizations similar to those condemned on university campuses. They were intense and brave protests against racial segregation, white supremacy, imperialism, and the Vietnam War. At the time, the promoters of civil rights laws were attacked and discredited as dangerous and violent.

Now, one of the most sensitive demands of the students, aside from the end of the massacre in Palestine, is the *divestment* of financial capital from *their* universities in the powerful war industry, which echoes the struggles of American students against another apartheid, that of South Africa. Their demands had repeated effects in the 80s, in the second decade of this century, and, more recently, in the effective negotiation of divestment from these industries by Brown University and Rutgers University.

Although the new law attempts a universalist language, it only mentions one protected group to penalize any expression "against Jews." Any criticism of the State of Israel or Zionism is now identified (by federal law) as antisemitism.

The law establishes a single, official philosophical criterion: *"The International Holocaust Remembrance Alliance's practical definition of antisemitism."* This organization has been repeatedly criticized for its equating of antisemitism with any criticism of the policies of the State of Israel and for its strategic conflation of antisemitism with anti-Zionism. Its *"practical definition of antisemitism"* until yesterday had no direct legal consequences. Now it does.

According to the law, *"Antisemitism is on the rise in the United States and is affecting Jewish students in schools, colleges, and universities from kindergarten onwards."* Which is true. But this phenomenon has not been a consequence of anti-colonialist activism or the left worldwide, but rather of the resurgence of neo-Nazi and neo-supremacist far-right groups that have expanded their influence in the government and who, as in Europe and Latin America, tend to be pro-Israel-at-any-cost. Just look at the libertarians in the United States, Brazil, Argentina, Italy, France, Ukraine, and other countries.

Similarly, freedom of speech protected by the First Amendment of the Constitution has once again shown what it has been since its adoption in 1791: the freedom of the white man, the rich man, the imperial slaveholder. When abolitionists tried to exercise it in the 19th century, they ended up harassed, persecuted, imprisoned, or lynched.

"The fight against this hatred is a national and bipartisan priority that must be successfully carried out through

a whole-of-government and societal approach." Police officers spitting on the Palestinian flag on campus, politicians claiming that Palestinians should be erased from the planet, rabbis stating that a Buddhist or someone who bows to Jesus must die for idolatry, is not hate speech or incitement to violence. The de facto and systematic annihilation and harassment of Palestinians is not hate speech because it is not speech.

Apart from an organized militia in the underground, like any colony, Palestinians do not have their own army. If they defend themselves using force, as common sense and the UN recognize as a right, they are terrorists. Besides, they do not exist. They are a product of the fiction of those who engage in "hate speech."

As members of Netanyahu's government themselves said, Palestinians do not exist and, moreover, they are the descendants of Amalek, which is why men and children must be exterminated according to a divine order given to the current Minister of Defense, Ben-Gvir, three thousand years ago. As Golda Meir said, "*we cannot forgive them for forcing us to kill their children*". But this is neither racism nor an attack on a human group due to their ethnic or religious origin. On the contrary, the law shields American politicians and the genocidal government of Israel from being accused of suppressing the existence of tens of thousands of children and other humans in Gaza because of Hamas—for some mysterious reason, Hamas' hostages never die under any Israeli bombardment.

The law was an achievement of legislative creativity, immunizing a specific group of human beings and omitting others. All calls to exterminate Palestinians, repeated endlessly by authorities, journalists, and religious figures, are not considered and are therefore not punishable. On the contrary, they are now protected from any criticism. Neither the International Criminal Court nor the International Court of Justice nor any law can infringe on the sacred and divine right of Israel to massacre a hundred thousand people in less than a year in the name of their blessed right to defend themselves against those who "attacked first."

For several generations, any reaction to this divine right is censored as terrorist. As Israel's ambassador Gilad Erdan said at the UN the day before: *"We always knew that Hamas hides in schools. We did not realize they are also at Harvard, Columbia, and many elite universities."* Shortly after, Senator Tom Cotton of Arkansas held a press conference denouncing the "little Gazas" on university campuses. Like Gaza, pro-Palestinian students suffered violent repression from the police and pro-Zionist groups.

That's why it must be punished there as well. The new law specifies that its goal is *"to expand the power of the Secretary of Education"* to give them the freedom to punish those who do not understand what the Government understands. Something similar will be done by the Supreme Court in 2024 by expanding the power and immunity of presidents, who are the ones who appoint the Secretary of Education and other ministers. The law concludes with the following phrase, reminiscent of a religious figure interpreting a sacred text: *"Nothing in this Law shall be subject to interpretation."* A century ago in Italy, this was known as fascism.

When someone is offended by protests against the massacre of 70 thousand people, more than half of whom are children and women, almost all (unjustly) unarmed, but is not bothered by the massacre of 70 thousand people, it speaks for itself without the need for explanation.

The Nazis not only shut down the historic Bauhaus School of Architecture, which they considered corrupt, but also declared the Theory of Relativity to be false because its author was Jewish, while banning thousands of books for being *anti-German*. Now, anti-Zionists. We continue to move closer to that same surrealism.

From now on, in the Greatest Democracy of the Free World, we will have to become more poetic and rely on metaphors, as in the times of Nero, who was referenced with the number 666 (his name in the Hebrew alphabet) because, while there was some freedom of expression, it was prohibited when it effectively challenged the imperial power of the time.

FORECAST: IF NOT BY LAW, IT WILL BE BY CANNON

CONTINUING WITH THE OBSERVATION of the formula $P = d.t$, we can deduce that in this century we will see an increase in the t of China and a gradual decrease in the t of the West or Euro-America due to the inverse balance of P_a and P_b (the West and the East)

$$P_a/t_a = P_b/t_b \text{ where } P_a < P_b \text{ and } t_a < t_b$$

The current ideological and geopolitical earthquake is pushing the hegemonic power to resort to all resources, proceeding, according to the formula $P = d.t$, through its three main steps: (1) narrative, (2) legal, and (3) military.

We will leave this issue for a future expansion of this study.

INDEX

FIRST NOTES

[II] Marx, Karl. *The American Journalism of Marx and Engels. A selection from The New York Daily Tribune*. Edited by Henry M. Christman. Introduction by Charles Blitzer. New York: The New American Library, 1966.

[II] Hobson, J.A. *Imperialism: A Study*. London: James Nisbet. 1902, p. 60.

[III] *William Lloyd Garrison's The Liberator*. 11 de setiembre de 2015.

[IV] *Abolitionists and Free Speech*. (2021). Mtsu.edu

[V] *Avalon Project. Constitution of the Confederate States; March 11, 1861*. Yale University. avalon.law.yale.edu/19th_century/csa_csa.asp

[VI] *Savage, Charlie. "Immunity Ruling Escalates Long Rise of Presidential Power." The New York Times. (Versión impresa: "Sudden Leap in Presidential Power's Long Rise.") July 3, 2024, Section A, Page 1.*

[VII] Tanno, Sophie. "Germany Demands New Citizens Accept Israel's Right to Exist." CNN, CNN, 27 June 2024, www.cnn.com/2024/06/27/europe/german-citizens-israel-right-to-exist-intl/index.html. Accessed 5 July 2024.

VIII "In 1945, George Orwell wrote an introduction to *Animal Farm*. It was not printed, and remained unknown till now". *The New York Times*. 8 de octubre de 1972, p. 142.

www.ingramcontent.com/pod-product-compliance
Lightning Source LLC
LaVergne TN
LVHW091217080426
835509LV00009B/1037